Helping Your Church Live Stream

How to spread the message of God with live streaming

By Paul William Richards

DEDICATION

To my Wife Lauren who renews my faith each and every day.

CONTENTS

ACKNOWLEDGMENTS

To everyone who helped solve a technical issue or provided guidance inside our **Churches That Live Stream** Facebook group (facebook.com/groups/church-streamers).

1 INTRODUCTION

Congratulations! You have felt God's calling to get more involved with the church's technology used for audio and video production. God works in mysterious ways. Maybe you have been a technology whiz-kid ever since you first started using computers. Maybe you are still trying to figure out how to use your very first smartphone. Either way, your church is interested in spreading the message of God and catching up with the times using live streaming. Everything on this earth and in our path is part of an intricate plan. You should be honored to serve God with your vocation, using the gifts he has given you to help others find faith through your church. Today more than ever before people around the world are connected online. Our world is changing rapidly creating new challenges and opportunities for ministry leaders. God has built a tremendous distribution network on the internet connecting the world like never before. It's an exciting time in history for ministers of the gospel to leverage advances in technology for good.

A friend of mine, Andrew Haley, the product evangelist for Wirecast, explained to me on a recent podcast how important technology has been to Christianity over the past 600 years. Haley explained "One of the main reasons why western religion has succeeded so greatly to this day, is because it has always taken advantage of emerging technologies… The medium isn't the message; it's the medium that you use to communicate the message. In the 1500s, we saw the printing press emerge, and bibles were being printed for the first time in history. We saw an explosion of what was being made available in written form, with new translations that were suddenly available all over the world… Over the past one hundred years, we have churches moving on to the radio with the early evangelical churches that have now moved into TV and televangelism… and now today we are moving into a new form of communication, where you can distribute your message on digital platforms using social media. The churches that are the most successful and most resonate with people are the ones delivering their message in the places that people are listening. Those who are producing content in a form that is consumable and makes sense in the day and age that we live in, we be to prosper from the fruits of new communication pathways."

After working with hundreds of churches, I have set out to create an easily digestible reference guide for ministry leaders who want to leverage the power of live streaming to embolden their message. This book will include a high-level overview of live streaming that answers the foundational questions and concerns about video production and live streaming inside the church. It will also include resources for online learning, a glossary of technical terms, and a narrative that provides perspective for volunteers, pastors and tech-geeks alike. After reading this book, ministry leaders will have a better understanding of the vocabulary, workflow and growth strategies for spreading the word of God with live streaming and digital media.

I like to think about live streaming as a bridge that can connect your church with the world. As you will uncover in the coming chapters, this bridge can bring your church closer to the elderly, shut-ins, and traveling members of your church. Many of these folks may not be able to attend your church on any given Sunday physically. Together we will discover why live streaming is much more than a simple window into your church on Facebook. It can become a strategy for increased communication, outreach and mindshare inside your local community and the world at large. Let's start with a look at how social media and live streaming has changed over the past ten years with a story about Village Lutheran Church in Ladue, Missouri.

2 TELL YOUR STORY

My story starts at Village Lutheran Church in Ladue, Missouri. Pastor Kevin Golden, is the inspiring and warm-hearted ministry leader at my wife's hometown church. Pastor Golden is on a Skype call with my wife and I, as he prepares us for our wedding ceremony planned for June of 2013. My wife had recently said "yes" when I asked her to marry me and start a new life in West Chester, Pennsylvania, over 800 miles from Ladue.

In 2013, not too many churches were live streaming their Sunday services. If you go back to the early parts of the 21st century, social media as we know it was still being invented. Facebook officially started in 2004, but for years the platform was only known as a place for college students to stay in touch with their classmates. Still, I found it technologically forward for Pastor Golden to provide us with marriage counseling over the internet.

Many historians will tell you that over the past twenty years, the world has experienced the greatest cultural communications shift in human history. Over the past ten years, what I like to call the "Grandmom Effect," has quickly turned Facebook into a website older generation use to keep up with their children and grandchildren. Social media has spread by the millions and eventually billions all over the world at unbelievable rates. Over the years, churches from every faith have started to use technology tools such as Skype

CHURCH
Pro Video Tip
Facebook is a great place to reach new members and accept digital donations. Make sure your Facebook Page is setup with the "Non-Profit" category.

and Facebook to stay in touch with members who have moved away from their hometowns, as my wife has. It has quickly become more and more common for churches to start using social media to keep up with current and new members online.

On June 6th, 2013, Pastor Golden married my wife and I in St. Louis, Missouri. It was a beautiful ceremony held in the backyard of my wife's childhood home, nestled in-between Concordia Seminary and Washington University. As my wife and I moved into our new home outside Philadelphia, Pennsylvania, we slowly lost our direct connection to Village Lutheran Church.

This is a story that so many people can relate to. It's always a hard process, leaving your hometown church for a life that is pulling you in another direction. It took a lot of "church shopping" to finally find a new church that we felt could fill the hole left behind in St. Louis. We still visit Village Lutheran once or twice a year on holidays. We have had our children baptized there, and we plan to keep a lifelong connection to the church.

It wasn't until 2018 that I had the foresight and the financial ability to help donate a live streaming system to the church. I reached out to the leadership at Village Lutheran Church to see what I could find out about regarding the current audiovisual system. I wasn't surprised to find out that there was an amazing audio system already in place that we could use with the new live streaming system. It also didn't surprise me that the existing camera system was analog and unusable. The timing happened to be perfect because the church was planning to put together a small IT team who would do a variety of things at the church. One of their responsibilities is now managing the live streaming system. By the end of 2018, we had put in place a live streaming system for Village Lutheran Church helping them spread the message of God and promote the unique programs they offer.

My wife and I had a personal interest in opening a window into the church for "transplant" families like ours. We were incredibly excited about the thought of watching Pastor Golden during the Christmas services. For my wife, the idea of imagining her mother and family in the pews on screen was captivating. We also wanted to help the church succeed in accomplishing its own outreach goals, which included growing its membership and adding additional service. That is where this book comes into play. This book is my attempt to provide a guide to churches interested in using live streaming to connect their church with the world.

My goal is to simplify the complicated world of streaming media. Inside this book, I will provide insights for ministry leaders who are considering the use of live streaming as an outreach tool. With a little strategy put into place, we can leverage live streaming as a communication bridge for the world to share and enjoy with friends and relatives that may span the globe.

After reading this book, you should be able to answer foundational questions about why so many churches have adopted live streaming technology. This book will provide perspective on best practices for live streaming church services and helpful reflections on real-life case studies from churches and pastors who are happily filling their pews with new members each week. We will talk in depth about setting up a digital donations strategy and enabling your social media accounts to accept donations directly through YouTube and Facebook.

This book will also include actionable checklists for ministry leaders considering live streaming at their church. I would encourage you to join our Facebook Group called "Churches That Live Stream" to see how other churches are embracing social media and live video streaming around the world. In the following chapters, it should be clear to you how your church can use live streaming and social media to reach new members and folks who may be bedridden or shut-in. An online training course accompanies this book for technology directors and volunteers alike who may become the next "champions" of your live streaming program. Our online training course also includes a PowerPoint presentation template you can use to present the benefits of live streaming to your church leadership.

CHURCH
Pro Video Tip

Join a group of over 500 churches on Facebook! This is an amazing place to ask questions and get honest answers! Join at
facebook.com/groups/church-streamers

I sincerely hope this book becomes a resource that is deserving of a place on your bookshelf or in the drawer of your media support desk. At the end of this book, you will find a glossary of terms that will help you and your team familiarize yourselves with the type of technological vocabulary frequently used in live streaming. I know for many pastors, learning this type of information is like learning a new language. I want to make this journey a walk in the park for you. Feel free to download the audio version of this book on audible.com and take a walk in the park as you listen.

Finally, this book was written to inspire readers to use modern tools to tell their organizations' unique story about their faith. At the end of the day, live streaming is just another storytelling tool helping organizations reach those who may need guidance, education, or simply a nudge in the right direction. Live streaming is so powerful because it can reach people from all around the world. Sean McDermott, the Production Director at LCBC Church in Marietta, Pennsylvania says "I am expectant toward the growth that will come through church online. God is doing some cool stuff through several groups that are participating with our gatherings from in their homes. The preparation and work to make that experience excellent each week is worth it for people to experience life-change through Christ outside of our buildings" (McDermott, 2018).

Social media has become a medium for empowering individuals to like and share the things they believe. We live in a world that is more connected than ever before. Understanding that everyone on earth is connected in some way, within six degrees of separation, will be an important stepping stone in our thinking about social media. Your church now has the power to reach people in large connected networks which include groups of family members and friends. These are the people that are most important and most influential in the lives of your church's current members and their extended online network.

I believe you will find that live streaming your church services will help you connect with people from all walks of life. Maybe you will reach people who have given up on church or think that the service isn't relevant to their lives. This is a fantastic opportunity to bring God back into the lives of so many people. But don't take my word for it. Let me start with a list of testimonials that are sure to inspire.

"Yes, we have folks check us out online long before they ever cross our doors. We also have shut-ins who will watch our services when they cannot make it to church." – **Scott Cundiff Clear Lake Nazarene Webster, TX**

"We have the best opportunity for the farthest reach with the Gospel via web streaming. We have members and nonmembers that view live our archived services." – **Roger Conant**

"We started live streaming one year ago, and we have already had real life results from it. On Facebook, we're seeing 20x the results of YouTube. One recent stream got over a 1,000 views on FB with many comments and dozens of shares." – **Doug Joseph, Christian Apostolic Church Shreveport, Louisiana**

"Yes, we stream our Chapel services at High Point University to allow parents from around the country and world to see their children take leadership roles in our services." – **Don Moore**

"It helps to introduce new people to the church, those members who are unable to attend services because of work, shut-in members, members who are studying

abroad, members who are out of the local area on business." – **Samuel Nelson**
St. **Bess**

3 STARTING YOUR DIGITAL MEDIA INITIATIVE

Starting a digital media initiative at your church can transform your organizations communication capabilities. Over 65% of Americans identify themselves as visual learners. Research now shows that foundational audiovisual tools can help increase what your congregation can effectively learn each sermon. A recent study on Audio-Visual teaching in colleges shows that 97% of students are interested in electronic teaching, 84% have a better grasp on the content, and 67% think audio-visuals enhance communication (Liang, 2006).

Howard Gardner has identified three different types of learning styles in his book "The theory of multiple intelligences" which was published in 1983. Considering each type of learning style can help your ministry better inform and connect with your community. A well-designed digital media initiative should embolden your existing services with elements that support each major learning styles (Gardner, 1989).

The first learning style is auditory. Auditory learners learn best with the spoken word, even if they are speaking out loud themselves. Auditory learners may be getting the most out of each service as they sing along with the choir and listen to the sermons. Auditory learners remember information best when it is accompanied by nonverbal sounds such as ambient synths, drums, or other musical backgrounds. Auditory learners may also internalize what they have learned best during an informal discussion in small breakout sessions.

Your church's digital media initiative should consider a plan to engage auditory learners with media that can support their best learning channels. Podcasts are a great way to support auditory learners. Once your services are being recorded it is possible to simply post the service in its audio-only format via a podcast. Another idea would be to have a curated podcast that reflects on certain segments of the service which will be discussed further along in this book. Auditory learners enjoy listening to podcasts while they are in the car, at the gym, or simply shopping for groceries. Engaging auditory learners within an audio-only format can help your church extend its communication capabilities greatly.

The next learning style is visual. Visual learners learn best when their visual senses are engaged throughout the learning process. Many churches have used overhead projectors with transparencies to engage the congregation's visual senses. Overhead projectors with transparency have often been used to provide visual cues for lyrics to songs. Visual learners also enjoy reading and feel an additional connection to the service when they can read along with songs during the service. Your church's digital media initiative can extend the visual learning experience with digital projectors that show bright and colorful imagery to supports the message of the service. Software such as Pro Presenter and EasyWorship help manage the process of displaying visual aids in the form of a curated presentation.

You can recognize visual learners because they will often sit in the front rows of your church. You may even hear a visual learner say "show me" as you explain something in a small group. Once your church starts to create visual presentations, you will notice visual learners will stay more engaged. Your church's digital media initiative can now include live video streams and recordings that include these presentations. Your digital media team may decide to mix together a live video camera feed focused on the pastor paired with the presentation being displayed on large projectors throughout the church. Using video production software such as OBS, Wirecast, or vMix, which you will learn more about in this book, your team will have the capability to mix multiple visual learning elements together and create short or long-form video content. Video content is by far the most effective format on social media platforms. Further along in this book, we will discuss how to effectively use your church's live video streaming system to create engaging videos for social media and your churches website.

Finally, the last learning style is Kinesthetic. Kinesthetic learners absorb information best when they are hands-on with what they are learning about. Kinesthetic learning inside the church involves movement, such as kneeling during prayer or the process of movement and taste during communion. You may have to get creative when finding ways to engage your congregation with the ability to touch, feel, and move during your service. Clapping is a form of Kinesthetic learning that can be accompanied by rhythmic movements during songs. This type of learning may happen best during group volunteering or missionary work. If your digital media initiative can capture the essence of Kinesthetic learning on video, you can share this video and connect with others who desire this same experience. Sharing with the world experiences that involved Kinesthetic learning is a powerful way to attract new members to your church.

Timothy Jackson, a leader in the digital media group at the University of Valley Forge says, "Digital media is one of the largest and fastest-growing majors here on campus." The University's mission is "to prepare individuals for a life of service and leadership" and Jackson says, "Digital media allows us to do this in a new medium… we have the opportunity to pour into our students and they get to use media for Christ." The University of Valley Forge began in 1939 and started its digital media program in 2007. The digital media group is now involved in over 25 projects a year, which include student-run video production for Christian based conventions, concerts, and festivals (Applied Video Technology, 2019).

As you consider how you will communicate with these various types of learners, your digital media initiative can support you. Increasing your ability to effectively communicate can be broken down into three important areas of interest. Think about your church's communication efforts with an emphasis on internal, social, and external goals. Internal communication is the experience inside the church. Your effectiveness here is crucial because it is the foundation for further growth via social and external communications. Internal communications embolden your congregation to unite under a common cause. Churches that fail to effectively communicate internally will have trouble building social and external movements.

Social communication is the next step for most small to medium-sized churches interested in spreading the message of God in their local and extended regional communities. The most effective form of social communication is word of mouth. Through the power of suggestion, emboldened community members from your church can effectively spread your church's mission with the power of the spoken word. By effectively communicating and providing the necessary tools to community members, word of mouth is one of the most effective communication tools. In today's age of the internet, your digital media team can create assets that your emboldened community members can share with their online networks of connected friends and families. Live video streams from complete sermons may be ideal for sharing a virtual window into your church, but shorter more concise video messages may also be effective. Research shows that videos are 1,200% more likely to be shared than pictures or blog posts. Consider having your digital media team record short clips of your live streams to be shared throughout the week.

External communications happen outside of your church. This type of communication is often highly sought after because it comes from the second and third-degree sources. Public Relations is the "practice of deliberately managing the spread of information between an organization and the public." Most churches do not budget for hiring a public relations company to manage this process, but with online social media, you can effectively manage the spread of information between your church and the public. This is where your church leadership will have to guide your digital media team. Some deep thinking will be required to set up the proper procedures and standards of practice for your digital media team to follow in order to make sure they are accurately representing your churches mission. Throughout this book, we will review best practices and present ideas that your church leadership should consider as you build out your "Digital Media Best Practices" guide. With great power, comes great responsibility. Your digital media team should understand the importance of effectively managing your churches external communications and its usefulness for connecting with home-bound parishioners, members of the church who are on vacation, new members, and younger generations.

4 BEYOND LIVE STREAMING: TWO WAY COMMUNICATIONS

Live streaming is generally thought about as a one-way broadcast from a single location to audiences around the world. For many houses of worship, this idea is a simple solution for sharing the message of God with a wide audience outside of the four walls of the church. With most one-way broadcasts, two-way communications is a privilege reserved for in-person members who are able to shake hands and exchange ideas in-person.

But today, everything has changed. The COVID-19 pandemic has literally shut down in-person church services around the world, to keep the deadly virus from spreading in large groups. Out of sheer necessity humans have been forced to communicate online. Live streaming a one-way broadcast helped churches to stay connected during difficult times and the technology provided pastors with a form of communication that could reach their dedicated congregation and beyond. Worship leaders helped to spread the message with emails, text messages, and phone calls sharing the live stream information as they provided members of their congregation's tips for staying connected even from home.

With each passing week, communities longed for the in-person experience they have grown used to at church. The need for fellowship and community engagement continued to grow as live streams lacked the two-way communications worship leaders, pastors, and families longed for. Forward-thinking worship leaders found video conferencing software such as Zoom and started to host meetings to keep their congregations connected even as everyone was distributed physically.

It was April 21st when Michael Begeman reached out to me from the *The Church of Conscious Harmony*, in Austin, Texas. Michael had been using a PTZOptics 20X-USB camera to live stream his churches services using OBS, but he had questions for me about using the camera with Zoom video conferencing. Michael had found that in the era of COVID, his worship leadership team had been spending a lot of time discussing how to best live stream their meetings and services to remote participants. Michael was thinking about social distancing restrictions, and what would happen when they are slowly lifted in Texas.

Would the church start to have both local (in-room) participants as well as remote participants during each worship service? When everything was a one-way broadcast, they only needed to produce a live stream of what was going on inside the church. But now they are having spiritual sharing and interactive conversations happening inside of Zoom. "What if you want interactivity?" Michael asked me. "How do you include remote participants in an interactive large class, workshop or the church service?" I took Michaels's questions very seriously and started a show called "Helping Your Church Live Stream (a weekly show)" to bring together worship leaders from all over the world who could meet once a week on Mondays to discuss these important topics.

"I can layout the journey for our church which has made it from all-local... to a 1-way broadcast with a mix of local and remote participants, to 1-way broadcast where everyone is remote, to finally an interactive all remote set up using Zoom," said Michael during our first live episode of the show. "Now we're thinking that when we can physically get back together, there's no 'going back' to the old way of one-way broadcasting and we will have to be including remote interactivity." The relatively good news Michael shared was the fact that his church's community was growing. "We've discovered during COVID that our community is much larger and more far-flung than we ever knew, so we feel the need to keep everyone included even when most of us can meet face-to-face."

Michael and his Wife were excited to meet many of the new members of their church using Zoom. They had particularly exciting conversations with people from all over the world during their small group spiritual sharing sessions they host online. Michael helped to lead a conversation about adding remote participants into the church's Sunday services. It introduces several issues that are more complex than having a 100% distributed church service online. Michael said, "Some of our classes and services are led by tech-savvy people, and some are led by people who need someone else to do all the technical legwork and moderation for them."

The idea Michael was trying to wrap his head around was a scenario where a class leader is sitting on the stage presenting. The presenters are seen by people in the room and by remote participants via Zoom. Inside of the Zoom meeting, Michael would like to encourage people to raise their hands and participate. Michael's team had already figured out some of the important Zoom moderation best practices which include (1) mute participants on entry; (2) disallow participants unmuting themselves; (3) restrict screen sharing capabilities to the host only; (4) disabling Annotation, Whiteboard, Chat, Participant Renaming, and Nonverbal feedback. In this way, the worship leaders can unmute participants who raise their hands, when they would like to share meaningful questions with the group. But here was the dilemma. When it's time for questions and sharing, the members inside of the church can raise their hands and pass around a hand-held microphone. But how does this work for remote participants via Zoom? Is there a way to allow the remote participants to have a conversation with folks inside of the church naturally?

This idea became the content of two very productive presentations made on our live show which are available to watch on our StreamGeeks YouTube channel. After consulting with audio technicians and multiple church media engineers, we came up with some simple solutions for bridging the technical gap between the in-person worship service and the remote participants on Zoom. The solution essentially requires some audio routing which is outlined in a free PowerPoint download at StreamGeeks.us/2way. There is a diagram below that Michael was nice enough to share.

Add remote participant interaction and amplification into the in-room audio

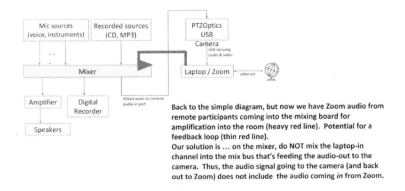

Back to the simple diagram, but now we have Zoom audio from remote participants coming into the mixing board for amplification into the room (heavy red line). Potential for a feedback loop (thin red line).
Our solution is ... on the mixer, do NOT mix the laptop-in channel into the mix bus that's feeding the audio-out to the camera. Thus, the audio signal going to the camera (and back out to Zoom) does not include the audio coming *in* from Zoom.

So what is the "new normal"? For a short period of time, it has become normal for ninety-nine percent of a church to attend remotely. There are billboards in Austin, Texas Michael tells us that say "the online church, it's a thing." Michael says "We enjoy the fellowship, we enjoy the, you know, what I called the warmer part of the church services... the hugging and all of that. You know, the breakfast that we have beforehand, but the new normal is that we're probably not going to have that for quite a while. Even as the social distancing restrictions start to get relaxed…. there are still a number of members of our community who are at risk in different ways." Because of age or other health-related issues, sadly many people will have to continue to participate with worship services online. So the question becomes, how do we include them as fully as possible, as active members of the community? As active participants in the interactive sessions in the classes and active members of the worship service. The goal has become to create a space where remote viewers can be on a peer to peer basis with everybody else who is participating in-person.

With all of this in mind, our team has created some new resources that are available for worship leaders who want to include remote participation in their worship services. One resource package is graphical, and it allows worship leaders to put a presenter full screen next to the remote participants shown in a grid-view using a software like OBS, Wirecast or vMix. These graphics are totally customizable for your church and available with tutorial videos included with the Udemy course for this book.

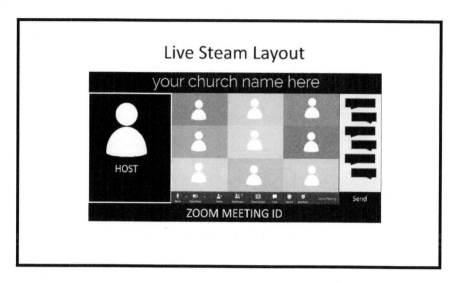

The first graphic, for example, has two primary uses. It has been designed to show a pastor next to their presentation, but it can also be transitioned to include another video source. This second video source could be someone providing sign language interpretations, or a speaker view of a Zoom conference. During some portions of the presentation, many churches may want to have the presentation next to the pastor but during other times it is helpful to show a grid view of the online participants from Zoom. In this scenario, production software such as vMix, Wirecast or OBS can be used to transition to another set up with this same graphics overlay.

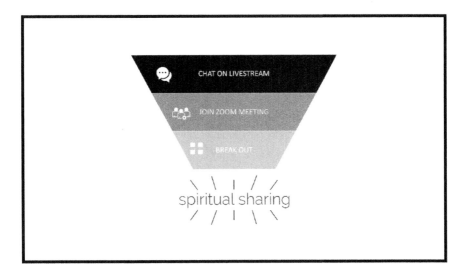

Finally, a high level look at how live streaming and video conferencing can work together is important for worship leaders to understand. The most likely place people will get notifications about your live worship service is social media. Your live stream is like a window into your church and it serves as the first-place people can engage with you live, in the moment. This is the first stage of engagement, but it's only one-way. Sure, it's nice to get prayer requests via a chat message. Even donations can be made through YouTube and Facebook. But ultimately, there is so much more you can do with two-way communications.

Using Zoom, you can have a moderator manage your online worship service. Therefore, you can leverage the power of social media, to encourage people to join your more intimate online meetings. Your worship leaders can moderate the online meetings and even allow participants to un-mute themselves and speak directly to your pastor. 93% of communications is non-verbal. Therefore, you should encourage members of your congregation to turn on their video and show face to the rest of your congregation.

When you start hosting worship services with an online meeting software you will likely find that there are a lot of people who want to join. In fact, you may even find members of your congregation are joining from outside of your local community. Zoom offers a great feature called "Breakout Rooms" which can be used to encourage small group discussions that can be used for spiritual sharing, organizational meetings, and Sunday school activities. This tool allows the meeting host to name and create small breakout meeting spaces that they can then send meeting participants to. It's a good idea to have your worship leaders set up as a host or co-host in your meeting so that they can manage who is sent to which rooms. Hosts also have the ability to broadcast a message to all break out rooms. For example, you may want to let everyone know that they will be joining the main group in just five minutes.

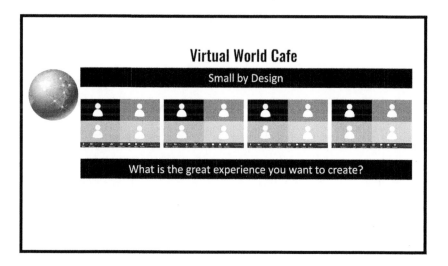

There are an unlimited number of ways to use breakout rooms to help your online services become more intimate sharing spaces. One exercise to try is called the "Virtual World Cafe." The Virtual World Cafe is a breakout session practice that separates the main meeting into breakout groups of four people. To do this, meeting hosts can randomly select to divide the entire meeting up into breakout groups of four. Groups of four are ideal, because they are small enough for people to get to know each other in a relatively short amount of time. Worship leaders can decide if they would like to have two or three rounds of these world cafe meetings, essentially shuffling the deck and setting up new breakouts.

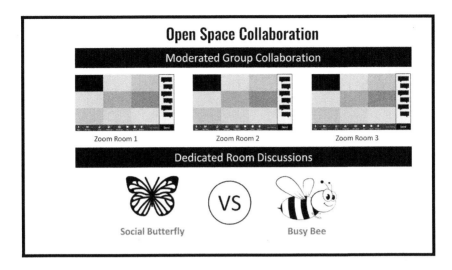

Another option for increasing communications for online worship involves multiple simultaneous meetings that are open for people to join at their own choice. This is more ideal for social butterflies who may want to jump from one meeting to another. Each Zoom meeting can be designed with a specific topic in mind and people can choose to move between these virtual rooms or dig deep into the conversation of a specific group.

Understanding that much of this technology is new, I have included new videos demonstrating this technology in the included online course. I can still remember joining my first Zoom breakout session, and it is going to be a learning curve for everyone involved. Perhaps the best way forward is joining our weekly live broadcasts and they evolve and change, you can take the parts that you find most practical and apply them to your worship services. Please feel free to ask questions in our online Udemy course if you come across something you would like explained in more detail.

5 WHAT SHOULD A COMPLETE NEWBIE KNOW ABOUT LIVE STREAMING A CHURCH SERVICE?

Houses of worship are unique spaces that require special attention to design and detail throughout technology upgrade projects. When it comes time to designing a live streaming system for your church, it's important to think about your organization's goals. If your media team is currently recording and editing videos of your services to upload to YouTube or Facebook, live video production may become a huge time saver. Bryce Boynton, the Audio Director for Flatirons Community Church in Lafayette Colorado, says "I am very excited that Flatirons is now live streaming services to the web. This has been a large undertaking because we have always post-produced services for the web. We have spent a lot of time contemplating how to maintain quality, but now in a live setting. The goal in this is to have a post-produced quality service by the time the last chord is played." Your church's online videos may very well be the first impression many potential members will see when they are "church shopping." A well designed live streaming system can eliminate tons of post-production work, while at the same time provide an experience your online viewers will love (Boynton, 2018).

The ideal church live streaming system should be simple enough for volunteer operators to use, but robust enough to create an engaging experience for online viewers. Putting yourself in the online viewer's shoes for a moment, the online experience should prompt a positive action such as sharing the video on Facebook or emailing a link to friends and family. When a viewer shares a live stream from your church, this opens opportunities for digital donations that can spread throughout their social media network.

Let's consider building the ideal church streaming system in 5 easy steps.

1. Leveraging existing equipment in the church
2. Selecting a video production switcher
3. Selecting cameras
4. Working with volunteers
5. Considering Christian music copyright law

Leveraging existing equipment in your church for video production

It's good news for many churches to find out that their investment in high-quality audio equipment can be used with a new video streaming system quite easily. In fact, in many cases, churches have more than 50% of the equipment they need for a new video production system when you consider the audio system that is already in place. For most systems, an inexpensive USB audio interface can connect the existing audio system to a new live streaming computer via USB. This way of connecting your existing church audio system to a new live streaming system is both affordable and intuitive. Most sound systems have an auxiliary audio output you can dedicate to this purpose. Your media team and audio engineers will be happy to find out that almost no changes to the in-house audio system will be needed to accommodate the new live video system. If you want to get fancy you can create a completely customized audio mix for your live stream. Some churches will go as far as adding "in-room" microphones to give the live audience a feel for the way the church sounds from the pews.

The next piece of existing equipment your church should consider using for a live video production system is an existing computer. Your church may already be using a computer connected to a projector or some type of large projection system to display lyrics and presentations. Thousands of churches are now using a free piece of software called the NewTek® NDI® (Network Device Interface) Scan Converter which can easily transport the video from a laptop computer into an IP based video stream sent over Wi-Fi or a hardwired ethernet cable. For many churches,

CHURCH
Pro Video Tip

You can make OBS look more like a professional switcher software by enabling "studio" mode. Go into settings and enable "ranchi" mode for an even more professional looking color theme.

wirelessly sending their PowerPoint slides back to a video switcher over their local area network feels like magic. That's generally because it's the first time they have ever used NDI. Throughout this book, we will mention numerous ways your church can leverage existing equipment and your LAN (Local Area Network) to save time and money when it comes to video production. Here we are in 2019, and there has never been a better time to get started with this type of live streaming equipment. Just five years ago, churches had to pay a content delivery network to stream their content to the world. Now live streaming is essentially free using Facebook and a smartphone.

If you are unfamiliar with some of the vocabulary used in this book, don't worry! We have a glossary you can reference, and an entire chapter dedicated to basic networking knowledge. We will focus on the NewTek NDI which was made to be plug and play, with only basic networking knowledge required for use. Leveraging your existing network will almost always be the most cost-effective way to add video sources inside your church. In the coming chapters, we will uncover a wealth of possibilities you can use to build a television quality production system on a budget.

Selecting a Video Switcher

When it comes time to select a video switcher for your church, an important thing to investigate is whether or not it supports the NewTek NDI (Network Device Interface). There is plenty of live video production software and hardware that supports the NewTek NDI including OBS, Livestream® Studio, Wirecast®, xSplit®, vMix®, and the NewTek TriCaster®. OBS, which stands for Open Broadcaster Software, is hands down the most popular live streaming software in the world because it's 100% free. If you decide to use OBS you will need to install the NDI Plugin

CHURCH
Pro Video Tip

OBS aka Open Broadcaster Software is a completely free live streaming software you can start out with.

It's available for download at www.OBSProject.com

available on Github to enable support for NDI (Open Broadcaster Studio, 2017). It's important to make the right decision when you choose a live streaming software because of how much time it takes to get comfortable using it.

Just like anything else in life, learning how to use new software is going to take time. In the beginning, you are going to be learning and doing things slowly. Eventually, you will start to get more familiar with the software and increase your capabilities in what is known as the "steep acceleration" stage. Eventually, your learning will plateau, and you will know enough to do anything you need to do inside your live streaming software or hardware system. Regardless of what software or hardware combination you choose, you will not want to throw away your time spent learning a video production software interface out the window. Take some time to consider the capabilities your church will likely require in the future, so you capitalize on your time spent learning how to use the software today.

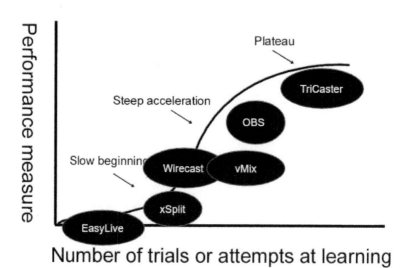

To help you make a good decision I have included a graph that mentions some of the top live streaming software. It covers how easy I found them to use, and the feature richness. I have used all of these software solutions, and I have to say churches are generally all over the map on their needs and the software they select. If you are unsure about your current and future needs, it's not going to hurt to get started with the free OBS software. Many of the basic principles you will learn in this software will benefit you if you decide to purchase a more feature rich, paid software in the future.

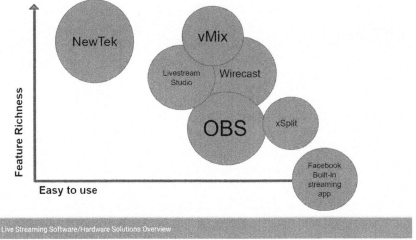

Live Streaming Software/Hardware Solutions Overview

Since OBS, Livestream Studio, Wirecast, vMix and xSplit all support the NewTek NDI, we can use these software systems for all sorts of video production scenarios that leverage your existing network. We already talked about easily connecting PowerPoint slides from a laptop computer directly into our video production switcher over Wi-Fi or a hardwired ethernet cable, but we can also send video out of our video switcher to additional monitors around your facility using the NewTek NDI. This means we can send high quality, low-latency video directly to overflow rooms and other spaces where we want to display the video output from your live stream. Lobbies, waiting areas, nurseries, as well as screens and displays in the sanctuary, are great examples of this. These are common places churches need to send video signals that used to be quite costly to access using traditional video cabling. Before IP based video production, churches would have to purchase expensive HDMI extension system and

CHURCH
Pro Video Tip

Wirecast supports the ability to import your work from OBS and upgrade your experience. This is a great way to upgrade from OBS to a more professional software.

run cables all over the facility. Now we can use a free Windows or Mac-based application called the NewTek NDI Studio Monitor, or any of the hundreds of NDI-enabled apps, to receive these video feeds on computers connected to our local area network. Generally, churches are using a miniature PC, or Mac computer (like the Intel® NUC or Mac Mini) connected via HDMI to the display and ethernet to the network. We will cover the networking required for this in more detail in chapter 10.

Selecting Cameras for your Church

When it comes time to select cameras for your church's live streaming system, one of the most important aspects to consider is an optical zoom. Many churches just starting will purchase a Canon or Sony camcorder with an HDMI output and connect that into their live streaming system using a capture card. Houses of worship are generally large spaces, and the need to zoom in from distances of 50 to 100 feet is common. Many churches are using PTZ (pan tilt zoom) cameras because they can be discreetly placed in hidden away locations and controlled remotely.

The best place to start when selecting a PTZ camera is measuring the distance between the location you want to put the camera and the object you want to zoom in on. PTZOptics® offers an easy to use online tool which allows you to calculate the dimensions of your camera image based on the optical zoom lens that you choose and the distance from the camera to your subject.

New Covenant
Church of
Malone, NY

Many PTZ cameras are now available with the NewTek NDI built-in, allowing churches to use a single ethernet cable to power the camera, control the camera, and send video & audio over the network. Using a PoE (Power Over Ethernet) network switch to connect the cameras to your local area network, will make the installation of these cameras incredibly easy. You will only be limited by the maximum length of ethernet cable supported which is generally 100 meters or 328 feet. A PTZOptics camera like the one pictured above can support traditional video output such as USB, SDI, HDMI, and RTSP video streaming. One simple way to get started with a laptop computer is to use a camera with USB. You can connect your USB webcam or PTZOptics USB camera to your laptop and pull the video feed directly into OBS or your favorite video production software. OBS is then used to live stream the video signal directly to YouTube or Facebook (Or both □). The main reason why many churches continue to select SDI and NDI connectivity over USB is because USB cabling is very unreliable when it's being extended over long distances. Ethernet and SDI cabling can easily be run hundreds of feet and still operate without fail.

You may decide to wall mount cameras at the back of your church. Generally, when it comes to wall mounting a PTZ camera, you want to make sure that the camera is high enough to provide a clear view over the heads of any church members sitting in front of the camera. You also have the option to ceiling or pole mount your camera to provide the best view for your online viewers. Many churches have high vaulted ceilings that are ideal for securely pole mounting a camera from the superstructure of the building. The picture above shows a church using the PTZOptics PTZ camera iPad app which is a popular wireless camera control solution for churches.

Working with volunteers

An important consideration for any church implementing a live streaming system is the fact that volunteers will be helping quite a lot. It's quite common to find church members interested in technology and video production who are willing to champion a media program within the church. Many churches encourage media programs with volunteer positions because it's a win-win situation for everyone involved. Volunteers in the church's media program can apply their experiences in the job market, and the church can benefit from their support. Generally, someone involved in the church's social media or audio-video team is the ideal candidate to help in organizing the church's live streaming efforts.

Bryce Boynton, the Audio Director for Flatirons Community Church, in Lafayette, Colorado says "One of the most important factors of effective team members here is leveraging their gifts. A lot of volunteers will start out saying; *I just want to help out wherever you need some help.* While this is a nice sentiment, not all people can serve in all capacities. We ask all new team members to spend a few weekends shadowing different positions to see what really makes their heart tick. Once we can identify together what skills and talents someone has, we'll train specifically to their strengths" (Boynton, 2018).

One entry level volunteering position is camera operation which can be made even easier with an intuitive PTZ joystick controller. You can have the entire live stream operated by just a single person who has experience operating the system. This person will be responsible for logging into YouTube and Facebook to retrieve the stream keys. They will also be responsible for opening the live streaming software and pressing the "go live" button. Once the system is streaming this person can focus on following the action with their remotely controlled PTZ camera(s). This could mean following the pastor with a PTZ camera or switching to the slides of a PowerPoint presentation. Depending on the level of complexity your team can handle, many software packages offer multiple ways to integrate with social media as well. This is a great opportunity to provide a useful job for volunteers interested in engaging with the online audience. It's always a great thing when you can display prayer requests, digital donations, and words of support on your live video stream. If a volunteer was able to communicate prayer requests directly to the pastor, this could become a fantastic position of communication between the online audience and the in-room audience.

CHURCH
Pro Video Tip

Consider putting a password on your Wi-Fi. Your church members may be consuming the bandwidth you need to broadcast. So password protect your Wi-Fi Access point during live broadcasts.

Working with volunteers at your church for your video production program is both rewarding and productive. Here is a short list of potential tasks volunteers can handle in the media production area:

1. Software setup including Facebook/YouTube stream key retrieval
2. Video switching
3. PTZ camera operation with an iPad, joystick or Xbox controller
4. PowerPoint / ProPresenter / EasyWorship song lyrics management
5. Lower thirds and titles management and queuing
6. Social media integration and comment queuing
7. Show scheduling, email distribution and group sharing

Resolution and Bandwidth

Resolution: 1920x1080p   Resolution: 1920x1080p
Bitrate: 2Mbps   Bitrate: 6Mbps

Available internet bandwidth can make or break your next live event. Bandwidth is measured in bits and the word "bandwidth" is used to describe the maximum data transfer rate of your internet connection. When we measure this speed, we are talking about megabits as they relate to time. One megabit = 1,000 kilobits and generally, we will talk about megabits per second which is the amount of data you can stream every second. Your internet speeds are measured in upload and download speeds. Megabits are used to measure the size of the bandwidth pipeline between your computer and the internet

Resolution	Pixel Count	Frame Rate	Quality	Bandwidth
4K 30fps	3840x2160	30fps	High	30Mbps
4K 30fps	3840x2160	30fps	Medium	20Mbps
4K 30fps	3840x2160	30fps	Low	10Mbps
1080p60fps	1920x1080	60fps	High	12Mbps
1080p60fps	1920x1080	60fps	Medium	9Mbps
1080p60fps	1920x1080	60fps	Low	6Mbps
1080p30fps	1920x1080	30fps	High	6Mbps
1080p30fps	1920x1080	30fps	Medium	4.5Mbps
1080p30fps	1920x1080	30fps	Low	3Mbps
720p30fps	1280x720	30fps	High	3.5Mbps
720p30fps	1280x720	30fps	Medium	2.5Mbps
720p30fps	1280x720	30fps	Low	1.5Mbps

Think about your live stream's resolution as the size of your live stream's canvas. The bitrate that you select is the amount of data that is used to fill that canvas. Therefore, you can have a high-quality 1080p stream with a bit rate of 6 Mbps, or you can have a low-quality 1080p stream with a bit rate of just 2 Mbps. Years ago, back in the time of SD (320x240 pixels), you could use flash to encode and stream at roughly 500 Kbps (That's half a Megabit). Today, most people will expect at a minimum of 720p video and a bit rate of at least 1.5 Mbps. New reports from Akamai show that most people watching 1080p video find that 6Mbps looks like excellent quality (O'Halloran, 2018).

The chart above displays various bandwidth choices you will have for your live streams. Using this chart and your available uploads speeds, you should be able to map out the number and quality of live streams your internet connection can support. A general rule of thumb says that you should only use half of your available upload speeds for live streaming (Download speeds don't help us with live streaming). Therefore, if you have 10 Mbps of available upload speed, you should only be live streaming with 5 Mbps. Leaving headroom in your upload speeds protects your quality of service from fluctuations in the internet connection which can cause interference with your stream's consistency. Keep in mind that most live streaming software will now allow you to live stream to multiple locations at the same time.

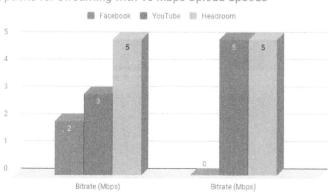

Options for Streaming with 10 Mbps Upload Speeds

Under certain circumstances you may need to choose between live streaming a single high-quality video stream, or multiple live streams of lesser quality. For example, if you have 10 Mbps of upload speed, you may create a 3 Mbps stream to YouTube and a 2Mbps stream to Facebook. If you are concerned about creating a single high-quality stream than you would only stream to YouTube using 5Mbps. Keep in mind that you can always record an incredibly high-quality recording to your local hard drive. Many production experts will record in "high bitrate" MP4 file ranging from 12-100 Mbps. The recordings saved to your local hard drive will always be of higher quality than the live streamed recordings available on YouTube and Facebook. The higher the bitrate you use, the larger your file size will become. I generally use between 8-16 Mbps for my standard video recordings.

If you are starting to learn about bandwidth and video storage, it's important to remember megabytes are used for files saved to a hard drive and megabits are used for streaming data on the internet. In my opinion, streaming in SD is no longer acceptable, and we must understand the bandwidth needed to stream in HD. The minimum resolution you want to live stream an event in would be 1280x720p with a 1.5 Mbps bit rate. 720p resolutions are technically considering "High Definition" but remember that the bit rate is the real measure of quality when we are talking about video. So before we talk about adaptive bit rate streaming and bandwidth calculations let's answer an important question. Should you be streaming in 720p or 1080p?

720 vs 1080

Both 720p and 1080p video resolutions are considered "High Definition". 720p is "High Definition," and 1080p is "Full High Definition." The quality of 1080p is generally considered better than 720p but it really comes down to the bit rate. Viewers will also need a 1080p display to watch the content. Most new mobile devices are capable of viewing content in at least 1080p quality. Streaming in 1080p gives your audience a choice to view the stream quality in 1080p or scale down to lower qualities as needed automatically. I also like 1080p for cataloging and archiving our videos in a quality that takes advantage of Full High Definition displays. At the end of the day, the higher the bitrate you use, the better the quality will look. So, a 720p 3Mbps video will look better than a 1080p 2Mbps video.

To answer this question for yourself, figure out exactly what your internet speeds are. You should be looking at your upload speeds. Once you know what your upload speeds are, try out multiple bitrates and see which look best. There may be compromises that you have to make. Maybe you can only live stream your services to a single destination? Maybe you can only support a 720p stream because you have an older computer? We will talk more about computer optimization and streaming solutions to maximize your quality in chapter 9.

Today most content delivery networks (CDN) are providing something called "adaptive bit-rate streaming." This technology takes the best quality stream you send and breaks it down into smaller resolutions and bit-rates for viewers with lower internet speeds to view in a reliable stream. CDNs such as YouTube and Facebook will use adaptive bit rate streaming to optimize the video quality your viewers receive based on their available internet access. This further supports the need to stream in the highest quality possible to allow the CDN to make the best choices for viewers on their platform. Some CDN's also call this process "Live Cloud Encoding."

A step by step guide to live streaming

1. Open your computer and check to see if the internet is working.
2. Schedule your live streams on YouTube and Facebook. Share the links out on social media and embed these videos on your website as needed. (Optionally your live streaming software may allow you to login to your CDN and start live streaming directly through the production interface).
3. Launch your live streaming software and check to see if all your cameras and audio sources are coming through properly.
4. Log in to either YouTube or Facebook and retrieve your streaming keys.
5. Enter your stream keys into your live streaming software and determine the bit-rates you will be live streaming in.
6. Start your live stream early and make sure you see the preview on Facebook and YouTube.
7. On YouTube, if you are using a scheduled stream, you will need to preview the stream before going live. You can click the go-live button whenever you are ready. On Facebook, if you have scheduled your live stream, it will start at the scheduled time automatically.
8. Check the chat room and make sure everyone is receiving your live stream properly.
9. If you are using social media integration, consider interacting with your audience. Answer questions if you can and display comments on the screen. Even consider thanking those who have donated during the live stream.
10. End the live stream when the service is over. Click the end stream buttons on both YouTube and Facebook. You can also click end stream in your video production software.
11. Turn off any equipment that will not be used until next Sunday.

12. Save your work if you have made any significant changes or improvements to your software configuration.

Church Copyright Licenses

When it comes to performing, recording, and live streaming Christian music, it's important that your church obtains the appropriate legal copyright licenses. Some of the Christian songs your church performs may be available for free under public domain. Public domain music is available to the public for free and therefore is not subject to copyright. You can find a listing of all public domain music here (https://www.pdinfo.com/).

While thousands of songs are available for free under public domain, many popular Christian songs require an appropriate license. Yes, copyright law can be quite confusing, but the good news is that the Christian Copyright Licensing International (CCLI), offers simple and affordable solutions for churches. The first license your church should have in place is simply called the "CCLI Copyright License" which covers the following activities:

1. Storing Lyrics
2. Printing Songs
3. Recording Services
4. Making Custom Arrangements
5. Projecting Lyrics
6. Translating Songs

This basic CCLI copyright license also includes two "add-on" licenses that can extend your church's legal usage of the music. The first is called a "Rehearsal License" which enables your team to share audio recordings via email and external worship planning software such as Planning Center, Onsong or ProPresenter. The second is a "Streaming License" which covers streaming and podcasting of your worship services. Keep in mind that these licenses only cover the usage of live-recorded audio. Therefore, you can only record music played by the musicians in your churches band. If your band plays with music tracks from other musician, you could be flagged for a copyright violation. All parts of your "live-recording" must be performed live or with copyright free materials. If your band is using a backing track or official recording from another band, you could get a copyright strike from YouTube or Facebook. YouTube and Facebook have an algorithm that listens to your content and decided whether you have included any copywritten content. If the algorithms find copywritten content, YouTube will start to monetize your video on behalf of the copyright holder by displaying ads. On Facebook, your live stream could be completely muted.

If your church is interested in using a live recording to create a CD this is covered under the basic CCLI license. In any given year, you can create and sell a number of CDs that is no greater than 15% of the maximum number of people in your CCLI license category. For example, if you are in the 500-999 copyright license category, then your church could only sell 149 CDs. You can only sell each CD for a maximum price of just $4. This portion of the license is intended to provide shut-ins members of the church the ability to listen to the church services music. The $4 CD price was created to help churches cover the costs of producing CDs for this purpose. If your church would like to create a CD for a fundraiser, you will need to purchase mechanical licenses for each song that you include in the album. Most mechanical licenses can be purchased for roughly $.10 per song per CD sold.

		Optional license add-ons		
Copyright License		Streaming	Rehearsal	Event License
Size	Base Cost (Annually)	Additional (Annually)	Additional (Annually)	One-time Cost
AH: 1-24	$61	$62	$87	$34
A: 25-99	$129	$62	$112	$54
B: 100-199	$216	$62	$138	$87
C: 200-499	$290	$89	$163	$117
D: 500-999	$407	$116	$214	$164
E: 1,000-1,499	$496	$168	$265	$198
F: 1,500-2,999	$602	$223	$316	$242
G: 3,000-4,999	$681	$276	$418	$272
H: 5,000-9,999	$859	$329	$520	$343
I: 10,000-19,999	$1,030	$435	$520	$413
J: 20,000-49,999	$1,370	$541	$520	$548
K: 50,000-99,999	$2,054	$806	$520	$823
L: 100,000-199,999	$3,466	$1,071	$520	$1,388
M: 200,000+	$5,582	$1,601	$520	$2,233

As you can see from the chart above, the pricing structure is based on the size of your congregation. From left to right we have the basic copyright license, a streaming add-on, a rehearsal add-on and a special license for onetime events. Onetime events include concerts, conferences or special meetings outside normally scheduled worship. The CCLI copyright license includes access to over 300,000 songs from more than 3,000 publishers. For example, here are the top 5 worship songs being sung in churches throughout the United States as of December 2018 (Christian Copyright Licensing International, 2019).

1. Reckless Love (Caleb Culver, Cory Asbury, Ran Jackson)
2. What A Beautiful Name (Ben Fielding, Brooke Ligertwood)
3. This Is Amazing Grace (Jeremy Riddle, Josh Farro, Phil Wickham)
4. Great Are You Lord (Jason Ingram, David Leonard, Leslie Jordan)
5. 10,000 Reasons (Bless The Lord) (Jonas Myrin, Matt Redman)

Working with the CCLI will make it easy and affordable for your church to obtain the legal rights you need to perform, record and live stream popular Christian music. If you already have a basic CCLI license and you plan to start live streaming, you should obtain the add-on streaming license. If your church has a special concert or conference, then you should consider purchasing a one-time event license. If you are going to be live streaming a special onetime event online, you will need to have the basic copyright license, the streaming add-on and the onetime event license. If you have any questions you can always call CCLI and speak with a representative (Christian Copyright Licensing International, 2019).

Once everything is setup your annual CCLI costs this will likely be put into your church's yearly budget. Once you have your CCLI license information it's a good idea to display the information on your website and in the default YouTube video description. You can have default information added to the end of each YouTube video you publish automatically by using the "upload defaults" feature inside the creator studio. On Facebook you can choose to display this information in your privacy policy link or at the end of your church's description area.

Privacy and Consideration

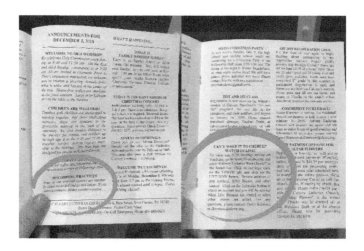

It's important to notify members of your church that you are recording and live streaming video inside the church. This can be easily done inside the weekly bulletin handouts and on your website's privacy statement. Calvary Lutheran in West Chester, Pennsylvania notes **"Some of our worship services are regularly video recorded and posted online. If you have a concern, please contact a pastor."** This information is available on the first page of every service announcements handout. This is an ideal way of notifying your churches members and acknowledging potential privacy concerns. If you have multiple services, consider live streaming just one of them to allow members the option of attending a service that is not being live streamed. Later, in the bulletin, it's a great idea to highlight members ability to view the live streams online.

Here is a sample segment from the weekly bulletin at Calvary Lutheran Church.

"Can't make it to church? Watch us Live! To view our 9:30 worship service on YouTube, go to the YouTube search bar and enter "Calvary Lutheran West Chester" in the search bar. Click on our Logo, click on the videos tab, and click on the LIVE NOW button. Browse archives of past services, Bible Boosts, and other content. Click on the Subscribe button and create an account to be notified when Live Streams are started or when other videos are added. For any questions, please contact the pastor."

CHURCH
Pro Video Tip

Bring the world with you on your next missionary trip using a LiveU Solo. These wireless live streaming devices allow your team to transport viewers to your missonary projects. Consider adding digital donations buttons to your next missionary outreach live stream!

Outreach programs and additional benefits

When you are considering a live streaming system for your church, it's important to think about the community and potential outreach programs that can benefit from your investment. Perhaps your video production system can be used to record a wedding for a family? Maybe you can use it to record baptisms and save the video recording for the families in attendance. A great way to share these videos with the members of your church is Dropbox. Sign up for a free Dropbox account and install the software on your live streaming computer. Have your video recording saved directly into a Dropbox folder which you can use to instantly share your video files with church members via email or text.

Many churches are taking their live streaming and video production technology on outreach programs around the world. Preparing your media team with video production equipment that can travel outside of the church can have many benefits. If you are interested in live streaming outdoors check out the LiveU Solo wireless streaming system. Many churches including my own, host outdoor services, especially in the summer. The LiveU Solo is a wireless streaming pack that can take an HDMI or SDI input and live stream it directly to Facebook or YouTube. This can allow your church to report on events that are happening outside the church and inside your local community. Is your church working with a local theater on an outdoor performance? Perhaps a parade or festival is happening in a location without internet access. The LiveU Solo will allow your church media team to live stream the event from anywhere that receives cellular service. The LiveU Solo can also be used to supplement your existing Internet and Wi-Fi access available inside the church.

YouTube vs Facebook for Live Streaming

Let's quickly talk about the major differences between YouTube and Facebook. As you can see, the church I go to, live streams directly to YouTube. When presented with a choice, most churches will choose YouTube because it does not require viewers to create an account the way that Facebook does. If we are purely concerned about the quality of the viewer's experience, then YouTube would win in a side by side technical comparison. The chart below compiles data from over 100 live streams that I have streamed to both YouTube and Facebook at the same time.

Live Stream Analytics Average

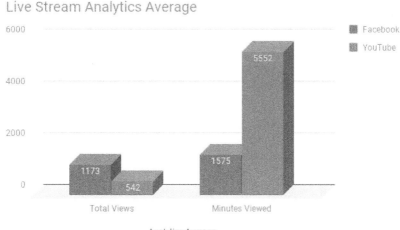

Analytics Average

In short, we have found that YouTube viewers will watch our broadcast over five times longer than on Facebook. This is a serious difference between the platforms which amounts to hundreds of hours of additional view time every week. On the flip side, Facebook is exposing our broadcast to larger audiences, sometimes twice as many unique viewers as YouTube. The main analytical points we looked at are total views, total minutes watched and average watch time. For our audience, YouTube is the preferred destination. The viewers who spend the most time on average watching our live streams, tune in on YouTube every week.

While some of our dedicated audience is watching on Facebook, we find that the average view times are lower because of the large number of "10-second views" Facebook records. Facebook is doing a great job at spreading our message, but on the whole, our dedicated audience has chosen YouTube for the premium viewing experience. Watching on YouTube is the choice most of our viewers make with the intent to watch for longer periods of time and there could be several reasons for this. I believe many people prefer the distraction-free, no login required experience on YouTube. I also believe that YouTube has built a reputation for high quality, reliable content delivery, that Facebook has yet to match.

YouTube Live Pro Tip: When you live stream to YouTube you have two options. You can schedule a live stream, or you can use the "Stream Now" feature. When you live stream to a scheduled event, all the views and view time are attributed to your on-demand video. When you live stream to your "Stream Now" channel **the view time is not attributed** to your on-demand video. Because YouTube's algorithm uses view time to rank videos, streaming to a scheduled post is a great way to start off strong on the platform and send YouTube a signal that your content has high viewer retention.

I believe that watch time is one of the most critical metrics for churches. But, if your church's current goals are focused on spreading the message of God to as many people as possible, Facebook can distribute to a larger audience than YouTube. So it becomes a conversation about **quality vs. quantity**.

	Total Views	Mins. Viewed	Avg. Watch Time	Location	Gender
YouTube LiveX	542	5,552	10:11	USA	Male
YouTube Product Line	557	4,136	13:13	USA	Male
YouTube Vid Summit	494	4,729	9:34	USA	Male
FaceBook LiveX	1,173	1,575	0:45	USA	Male
FaceBook Product Line	431	781	0:54	Europe	Male
FaceBook Vid Summit	341	819	1:13	USA	Male

There was a time when I thought YouTube live streaming offered everything we would ever need. **Why start using Facebook when we already have a reliable free option with YouTube?** Well, after two years of using Facebook Live streaming, I have to say, the platform has a unique audience and powerful tools I couldn't imagine living without. The advertising platform is possibly the best in the world, and the live streaming service is growing in popularity on a massive scale. It would seem like the best option for almost every church is live streaming to both platforms. If you have a weekly service, you may find out that your core viewers will prefer YouTube.

If you have an event based live stream, you may find that Facebook's reach is unrivaled and boosting the post is incredibly affordable compared to other forms of advertising. The only true way to figure out what will work for your church is to start testing things out for yourself. Doug Joseph, from the Christian Apostolic Church of Shreveport, Louisiana says "We started live streaming a year ago, and we have already had real-life results from it. On Facebook, we're seeing 20x the results of YouTube. One recent stream got over 1,000 views on Facebook with many comments and dozens of shares."

> **Facebook Live Pro Tip:** Facebook has many unique features that encourage churches to live stream exclusively to the platform. One feature is the Facebook live map, but it only works when you are using the Facebook live streaming API. The more live viewers you have, the larger you will show up on the live map. This is a great way to attract additional viewers. Facebook polls are another feature that is available exclusively for streaming on Facebook.

Remember that people watching online may initially be unfamiliar with your church. There are many things you may take for granted that could be foreign to your online viewers. Consider creating a presentation of introductory materials that explain the purpose of worship and the location of your church. These introductory materials will help orient your online audience and help plant seeds that can grow into a meaningful experience. These looping presentations can also be supplemented with introductory and closing remarks from your pastor filmed on video. In this way, your pastor can address the online audience directly without having to do so during his normal Sunday services.

Every church is different, and new technologies are coming out all the time. Popular trends include a shift toward IP based video production and automated camera controls with pan, tilt and zoom capabilities. Smaller churches are now able to put together high-quality video production systems on a surprisingly lower budget than ever before. Making an educated decision is important, and I have developed multiple completely free live streaming and video production courses to help support your learning efforts. You can find my courses all about church video production on UDEMY.com by searching for "church streaming" or following the links below.

Additional Learning Resources:

Church Streaming Course: https://www.udemy.com/church-streaming

Live Streaming Weddings Course: https://www.udemy.com/live-stream-weddings (Free Coupon Code: WEDDING)

6 MY FAVORITE SOCIAL MEDIA TIP FOR CHURCHES

The entire staff at your house of worship works each week tirelessly to produce an amazing experience that lasts for only a few hours on Sunday. Take advantage of this opportunity to make the most out of your hard work and get your message out to the world with live streaming. Whether you are simply rebroadcasting a church service that you recorded earlier in the day or live streaming the event in real-time, it's a great way to increase your church's exposure on social media. Capture the moment for your church members to cherish for years to come.

Here is a tip that many churches are taking advantage of to help spread the good word. Your target audience is likely local people who are friends and family of the dedicated members who currently attend your church every Sunday. Take advantage of that, and use the geolocation tagging feature available on Facebook for sharing the whereabouts of your fellowship every Sunday! During services, you should encourage your members to check into your house of worship on Facebook. When they do this their family members, and friends will be notified where they are, which just so happens to be at your church.

This is a great way to organically spread awareness about your church through the people who support you most. When people on Facebook see this "Check-in" post, it's likely that they are going to click the link to your church's Facebook page. If you are live streaming the service, they will be able to instantly see inside the church and imagine their friends or family members attending church right there! These are the types of experiences that push online viewers to attend church in person through social encouragement. You can encourage the people who may initially be hesitant to come to your church to get in contact with you.

Facebook truly is a social media platform that connects people with the things they like. The more people that like your Facebook page, the further your organic reach will become. Facebook has a map of all live streams that are going on at any given time. Look at the Facebook live map on a Sunday morning at facebook.com/livemap. It will be a true eye opener when you see the largest live streams on the planet are churches from all around the world that are amassing large audiences of online viewers. Combine the massive distribution and scale of this network with its newly created digital donation features, and you are looking at some very powerful new ways to spread the message of God and grow your church.

Here are ten tips you can use to grow your audience on Facebook.

1. **Video Production** - There is a HUGE need for professional video on Facebook, especially live video. Throughout this book, we will review how to increase your video quality and break through the clutter with the message of God.

2. **Take yourself seriously** – Develop your niche and listen to your audience. Be prepared to take constructive criticism and use it as fuel to grow.

3. **Be dedicated to your community** – You are dedicated to your local community. Can you extend this thoughtfulness to the online audience? Can you spend 20 minutes replying to comments after each sermon?

4. **Page growth** – Organic growth will happen over time. Collaborate and share your content with like-minded organizations. Don't forget to link to your Facebook page from your website and vice versa.

5. **Page Likes** – Facebook page likes are very similar to YouTube subscribers. "Likes" are used by Facebook to determine the interests of their users. Once someone has liked your page, they will be notified about your upcoming live streams. When someone engages with your live stream, Facebook will allow you to invite them to like your page. After each live stream, go back and click the list of people that engaged with your video. You can click the "invite" button to invite them to like your page.

6. **Email your audience** – It's important to maintain a line of digital communication with your congregation in this day and age. You should consider prompting viewers of your live stream to fill out an online form. In this way, you can collect your online audiences contact information and send them reminder emails about your upcoming events and live streams.

7. **Promote engagement** – You already have amazing services. Have you considered asking for people to engage? This can be done directly on your live stream with a lower third graphic overlay that says, "Click the love button if you love this sermon." This will tell Facebook that your audience is very engaged with your content.

8. **Native video** – If you can only live stream to one platform, you may want to choose YouTube. Many churches choose YouTube because you do not need to have a login to view the service. If so, remember to record or download your service and upload the video directly to Facebook. In this way, you are uploading "native" video content to Facebook which performs ten times better than simply linking to a video on YouTube or Vimeo.

9. **Boost your posts** – It's amazing how affordable advertising on Facebook is. There are entire books about advertising on Facebook, but the simple fact is that it works. I would suggest boosting your Sunday services for $5-10 each week and selecting the audience of people who already "like your page and their friends." This will send out the weekly service, with a donate button, to an extended network of people who already like you and their circle of friends. Facebook will notify friends of friends, that their friends like

your page. It's an incredibly great way to spread the word about your church and the people who support you.

10. **Have fun**! – There is something magical about light-hearted fun. Yes, we need to take ourselves and the people around us seriously. But we also need to make sure we are emitting a certain level of enjoyment in our work. Laughter is contagious, and fun will speak volumes when you are low key convincing new people to check out your church.

7 WORKING WITH VOLUNTEERS

Working with volunteers is so essential to most church streaming projects that the entire system is often designed to support them. This means that everything needs to be straightforward. The KISS (Keep it Simple Stupid) principle says that we should only add as much complexity as is needed to get the job done. You should only add additional equipment and production capabilities once your team is comfortable and ready for new challenges. Simply having members of your team read through this book can help jumpstart their understanding. Consider having your team listen to the audio version in the car on their way to church. This is a great way to increase their capacity to do more for the church when it comes to video production.

Making sure that your volunteers are ready to go when you need them can take some upfront planning. Make sure that they understand their responsibilities and have a general understanding of the equipment that you have in place. Maintaining an up-to-date wiring diagram with all the equipment your church is using can increase transparency and help your team understand what they have access to. You can create diagrams using PowerPoint or Google Slides that teams can share and collaborate on. I like to keep a three-ring binder that includes all the essential equipment manuals in one place. Having regular meetings with your volunteers on days other than Sunday is always a good idea. Building up lasting relationships with your volunteers will be the key to success. John Basile from the Stream Dudes notes "Assign production roles to anybody assisting with the production. This is very important with amateur and volunteer production teams as it allows specific people to "own" a part of the workflow. Assigning roles makes it easier for people to

CHURCH
Pro Video Tip

Consider posting a request for volunteers in your weekly announcements hand outs. You might be surprised who responds learn critical broadcast elements of a production, without overwhelming them. It will lead to better broadcasts and accountability on specific tasks."

Reach out for advice

Always remember that if you are overwhelmed from a technology perspective, you can always reach out for advice. Consider posting a question in the "Churches That Live Stream" Facebook group and get help from a fellow church media team member. It can help to visit another church in your area that is already broadcasting their services. Simply check out Facebook pages of churches in your area and see who has published a live stream recently. The Facebook live map is a great place to zoom into and check out on a Sunday morning. Consider reaching out through a neighboring church's Facebook page. Don't forget to compliment them on their recent live stream's video quality and ask for an introduction. Make a phone call and see if you can set up a tour of their facility. Bring some people along from the leadership at your church and invite some of your volunteers. After your visit, you should have a good idea of what you can implement back at your church. I have also included multiple church video production system walkthrough videos in our included online church streaming course. If you would prefer an online tour of a church streaming system, check out our YouTube channel and search for "church streaming system" to see what other churches are doing with their systems.

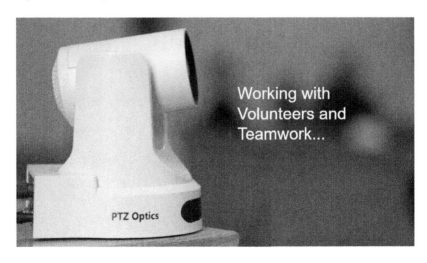

Working with Volunteers and Teamwork...

PTZ Optics

Most churches start with just one or two cameras before things become more complex to manage. Simplify your workflow in order to make it easier to identify a problem when one arises. When you do find a converter or adapter that you absolutely must use, keep a spare on hand in case one breaks. Kevin Amos Schmuhl, a church media director from Jamestown, North Dakota says "Avoid HDMI like the plague due to the HDCP copy protection protocols on that format. SDI is your best bet for reliability and quality. NDI is great but only if you have the networking chops to build out the networking infrastructure to handle it."

Another tip for growing your church media team is asking for volunteers in your church's service bulletin handouts. This is a great place to post your email address and make a public request for volunteers. If your team has regular meetings, you can note those here as well. I would highly suggest including this information along with or next to the section about where members can find out more about the live streams.

8 AUDIO VISUAL TECHNOLOGY BASICS

Now that we have come this far, I want to make sure we talk about some basic audiovisual principles, devices, and cables. Perhaps the most important basic principle of audiovisual is that **audio is the foundation of everything**. If your audio is somehow not in order, there is no amount of amazing video that will save your video recordings or live streams from complete disaster. The great news for most churches is that the in-room audio system you already have installed will work perfectly when connected to your live streaming and video production system.

Audio

Let's start with audio since it is so very important. The audio board is essentially the heart of your audiovisual system. Someone from your church generally has a good understanding of how it works. Most churches label every input of their audio mixer allowing operators to quickly identify which audio input they are working with at any given time. These inputs range from gooseneck microphones on the podium to wireless microphone receivers which correspond with microphones given to the pastors and on-stage talent. Audio mixers also include many audio outputs that may be used for powering speakers inside the church, sending audio to remote locations, and sending audio to your live streaming computer. These audio outputs can be used with either XLR or quarter inch (1/4") audio cables which can be either stereo or mono. If they are stereo outputs, this means that they have left, and right channels separated, and you will need to use two cables to get a balanced audio signal. If they are mono outputs, this means that

CHURCH
Pro Video Tip

Audio is always the most important part of any live stream. When setting up a professional audio system, consider consulting with a professional. You will find setting up the video side of things is much easier to do yourself.

both the left and right audio channels are paired into a single cable.

To bring these audio output cables into your live streaming computer, you will need a device called a USB audio interface. You can purchase these for under $50, and they take your main audio mixer's XLR or ¼ inch audio cables and convert them into USB. Now you can bring in the audio from your USB audio interface directly into your live streaming software in the same way that you would connect a USB webcam. In an upcoming chapter, we will cover audio in more depth. But for now, understand that you can easily work with your existing audio mixer to bring all your audio sources directly into your live streaming computer. Also, know that audio engineering and audio mixing is considered high art in audiovisual technology. Therefore, it's important to consult a professional when you are setting up a complex audio mixing system for your church. Take care to remember the easy things such as replacing the batteries in your wireless microphones before every Sunday. Once your audio system is all set up, you should be in good shape, and the system will require minimal support.

XLR Cables   1/4" Cables (Guitar Cables)   3.5mm Cable

Audio Software

Churches with a live band have much more complex audio system requirements. The band leader will generally take responsibility for the audio system integration which is shared with the pastor for in-room audio amplification. It is now popular for church bands to use a digital audio workstation software, also known as a DAW, to enhance the band's performances. Popular DAW software includes Ableton Live, Pro Tools and Logic. These programs run on a Windows or Mac OS computer and provide tools for band management such as backing tracks, click tracks, and audio prompts.

I have heard nothing but good things about church bands that use DAW software to increase on stage communication and backing musical support.

Ableton Live has become an industry standard for live performances, and many churches throughout the world use it. Doug Lawes from the Keys Vineyard Community Church in Big Pine Key Florida has helped me put together a video about his audio-visual system which uses Ableton Live as the "workhorse" of his system. Doug can program Ableton Live each week for the songs his band plans to play on stage. For Keys Vineyard Community Church, the musical performances made by the band each week are a central highlight for the service. Ableton Live is used to sync up the entire band using a click track to the tempo of the song. This click track is made available to each band member wearing an "in-ear monitor" headset. The in-ear monitor headsets can include tracks of spoken words that prompt the band such as "Chorus One in 3,2,1... Verse 2 in 3,2,1." Ableton Live is also used to synchronize the lighting system to display the correct colors and light movements throughout the performance. The Keys Vineyard Community Church is even using Ableton to sync up the lyrics that are being displayed over camera video outputs. I highly suggest watching our online YouTube videos with Doug Lawes to learn more about the ways he uses Ableton Live throughout his church services.

Just search YouTube for "**Professional Church Streaming | An Interview with a Pro - Doug Lawes.**"

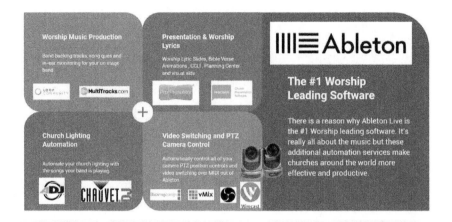

The diagram above shows just how essential audio can be to the entire audiovisual system in an interesting way. The music tracks can become the clock which the digital audio workstation uses to trigger other audiovisual systems in time. As you can see here, Ableton is used to enhance the music production by integrating with companies that provide backing tracks for popular Christian music such as MultiTracks.com and the Loop Community. These companies can provide songs with multiple tracks allowing your church band to "fill in their sound" with instruments that they may not have a member available to play. Ableton is also being used to automate song lyrics than can be displayed on top of the live camera feeds shown throughout the worship space, using software such as ProPresenter or EasyWorship. Finally, you can see that Ableton Live is being used to automate the control of church lighting and even PTZ cameras. All of this is quite advanced, but I found it important to note how powerful audio production software can be inside a church where music is so very central to the service.

Video

Ethernet Cable   HDMI Cable   SDI Cable

On the video side of things, I want to familiarize you with many of the cables, connectors, and devices that you may come in contact with as you build out and support your audiovisual system. Many of us are very familiar with HDMI, but a lesser known cable that is equal in importance is called SDI. HDMI stands for High-Definition Multimedia Interface. SDI stands for Serial Digital Interface. These two video cables have been the standard for transporting video ever since I have been working in the video production industry in 2008.

In recent years, a major upgrade in technology known as "IP based Video Production" has been sweeping the industry. IP based video production uses regular ethernet cables to transport video signals reliably over a local area network (LAN). IP technology is so important that I have dedicated Chapter 11 to review this topic in more detail. I also have an entire course that you can take for free on the NewTek NDI available on UDEMY.com for further learning. For now, let's clarify the different types of ethernet cabling.

Ethernet cabling and CAT(5, 6 or 7) cables are generally words used to reference the same thing. Ethernet cables come in a variety of quality levels which have to do with the maximum bandwidth and distances these cables can be used to support. Cat 5e is the most commonly used ethernet cable for video production. This is because Cat 5e is relatively inexpensive and it supports a full gigabit of bandwidth. A gigabit of data is generally more than enough bandwidth to transfer professionally compressed video signals. For comparison, a 3G-SDI cable can support up to three gigabits of data which is ideal for uncompressed 1080p high definition video at 60 frames per second. Since Cat5e cabling only supports one gigabit of data, it can only be used for 1080p60fps video when it is compressed. With the recent advancements in compression technology, gigabit ethernet has opened a whole new world of possibilities. It's normal to have slightly compressed 1080p video transfer at bandwidths of just 100-200 megabits per second. A new technology known as NDI-HX is a high-efficiency compression that transfers 1080p60fps video at only 12 megabits per second. This allows you to send multiple sources of HD video down a single Cat5e cable. Let's look at the details regarding various qualities of ethernet cabling below.

Cable Name	Bandwidth	Maximum Distance
Cat 5e	1 Gbps	328' (100 meters)
Cat 6	1 Gbps	328' (100 meters)
Cat 6a	10 Gbps	328' (100 meters)
Cat 7	10 Gbps	328' (100 meters)
HDMI 1.4	10.2 Gbps	50' (15 meters)
HDMI 2.0	18 Gbps	50' (15 meters)
SDI	270 Mbps	1000' (300 meters)
HD-SDI	1.5 Gbps	300' (90 meters)
3G-SDI	3 Gbps	200' (60 meters)

I have included the chart above as a reference tool you can use when you are thinking about running video cables. Churches are generally very large spaces and running a cable to a camera mounted inside the church can require upwards of one hundred feet of cabling. One major benefit of ethernet cabling is its ability to provide data and power over a single cable. This means that you can run a single ethernet cable to a camera which can power the device, control the device, and provide an audio/video stream. Therefore we are dedicating an entire chapter of this book to the power of networking. In the years to come, traditional HDMI and SDI video cabling will slowly start to make way for the world of IP. But the major roadblock to success is usually just the lack of networking knowledge available to the public.

Another benefit to ethernet cabling is how easy the cable is to make. Your volunteer team can easily create ethernet cables at custom lengths for your next project without the need of expert soldering tools. Ethernet cabling can be purchased in standard lengths or bulk boxes for larger projects. Your team can use simple crimping tools at each of the cable for convenient non-technical installation.

Capture Cards

Now that we have talked about cables let's talk about video hardware. I consider capture cards to be one of the most important tools in a video production tool bag. Capture cards come in all shapes and sizes, but generally, these devices take a video signal and convert it to USB. Usually, these devices will take an SDI or HDMI video signal and convert it for use with USB 3.0. This allows you to quickly connect your live streaming computer to another laptop, camera, or other video device and bring it into the computer and software you are using. Capture cards are a great way to get started on a budget because they cost less than $300.

Many churches that want to have multiple cameras will install professional PCIe capture cards inside a custom-built computer. These capture devices are called PCIe capture cards. PCIe stands for "peripheral component interconnect express," and they allow you to put multiple video inputs and outputs directly inside your very own custom-built computer. Most video professionals know that building a custom live streaming computer is the most cost-effective way to get the best "bang for the buck." While it may seem daunting to build a custom computer, you will save thousands of dollars by doing so when you compare it to the cost of off the shelf live streaming systems. If you are going to need more than just one or two cameras, I highly suggest building a custom computer with a PCIe capture card. Another way to get started with a multi-camera system is to consider a solution like the PTZOptics Producer Plus Kit. This kit includes a super-fast Intel NUC computer with an external PCIe card solution that supports up to four cameras.

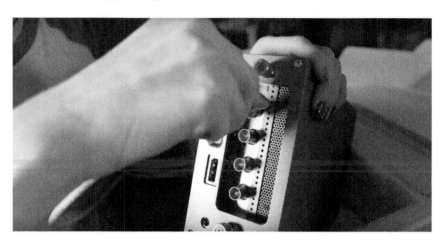

Video Distribution

Getting video into your live streaming software is the easy part. Extending the video from your live streaming computer to multiple displays throughout your church is where things can get a little more difficult. A very popular way to distribute video inside a church is an HDMI extender. HDMI extenders usually use CAT 5e cabling to extend HDMI signals long distances with transmitter and receiver boxes that provide HDMI inputs and outputs at either end. There are multiple types of devices used to design a video extension system, and I have prepared the chart below for your reference.

Extender Types	Purpose
Video Matrix	Takes in multiple inputs and sends out multiple outputs
Video Switcher	Provides video mixing capabilities with single or multiple inputs and outputs

| Video Extender | Extends HDMI or SDI video generally over ethernet or fiber cabling |
| Distribution Amplifier or Splitter | Takes a single input and send out multiple outputs |

There are so many unique needs for churches to display video throughout their facilities that the above reference chart should be useful. In our chapter on networking, we will also review new ways to distribute video over your local area network which may very well be the most cost-effective way to extend video across your facility.

Finally, I want to mention some of the popular cameras and controllers used in many churches. We already mentioned why PTZ cameras are so popular inside churches. They are discreet, and they provide a powerful optical zoom which is useful in large spaces. Still, in higher end video production systems, you will find traditional "over the shoulder" style cameras mounted on tripods with camera operators. Most PTZ cameras are controlled over ethernet. The simplicity of running a single ethernet cable to a PTZ camera to power, control, and capture video is a real technological breakthrough. This is becoming so popular, most live streaming software companies are including built-in PTZ camera controls right inside their software interfaces. Some notable software providing integrated PTZ camera controls include: OBS, Wirecast, vMix, Livestream Studio, MimoLive, and the NewTek TriCaster. With integrated camera controls your volunteers can view an organized collection of pictures that each represent exactly where the camera will go inside your church when the picture is clicked. This allows churches to cover various locations inside the church with a small number of PTZ cameras. It also allows the entire system to be operated easily by a single volunteer.

Still, many churches like to provide volunteers with an intuitive joystick controller. Joystick controllers are ideal for video production desks because they represent a valuable job for a volunteer. If you are looking to grow your volunteer team, having a dedicated joystick operator can add a lot of production value to your videos. A single joystick controller can control multiple cameras, and with a little teamwork, volunteers can capture an entire church service with relative ease.

Production Software

Finally, on the video side of things, we must consider our pastor's presentations. I am always surprised by how many churches still use an overhead projector with transparency slides. It's a distant memory, but I can still remember seeing transparencies used with a piece of paper placed on top to hide the unsung verses. Many churches have moved over to PowerPoint which is great because the software is incredibly straightforward. Unfortunately, I still hear from pastors who say they are spending more time preparing their PowerPoints than they do preparing for the sermon. This is where worship presentation software like EasyWorship and ProPresenter have saved the day. Modern worship presentation software now includes resource libraries full of Christian songs and Bible scriptures available in a searchable database. I enjoy working the drag and drop scheduling features for presentation arrangement that are designed for worship spaces. I find that dedicated worship presentation software will minimize the amount of time volunteers and pastors will need to spend organizing song lyrics especially. They generally make the entire presentation look and feel more professional as well. An interesting feature you may want to check out is called the "Foldback". Dan Willard from EasyWorship says "The foldback (aka, stage monitor or confidence monitor) is a separate output that comes from the computer to a monitor on stage or at the back of the sanctuary for everyone on stage to see. It includes elements of the presentation that are not on your main congregation display like a clock and the next line or item view." This is a great way to increase communications between your on-stage pastor and the church media team's operator. Dan says "It can also include service start and end countdown clocks. If the operator ever gets to the next slide late, it's okay because you can already see what line is coming up next" (Willard, 2018).

There are a couple of different ways you can incorporate your presentations into your live streaming software. The easiest way is a simple PowerPoint import. vMix supports this type of simple integration but some software, like OBS, does not support PowerPoint imports. EasyWorship and ProPresenter support NDI outputs which can easily become an input into your video production software. In some cases, you will have to use a "Desktop Capture" to pull in your presentation from a secondary monitor on the same computer. To do this you can use a desktop capture input inside your live streaming software. Using this option, you can choose which screen you want to capture. This will bring in a video input into your software that will mirror whatever you have currently on the selected display. To do this, many churches will dedicate an entire screen to PowerPoint. As the church service switches focus from the PowerPoint slides, the video production team may decide to switch to live camera feeds and other video sources that are available to them.

In the next chapter, we will review the audiovisual system installed for The Olivet United Methodist Church in Coatesville, Pennsylvania. This church has an audiovisual system that uses quite a few of the techniques we have talked about thus far. The next chapter will shed light on a real-life case study for sharing the good word of God with live streaming.

9 A LOOK AT THE OLIVET UNITED METHODIST CHURCH

I have had the distinct pleasure of working with Pastor Johnson of The Olivet United Methodist Church in Coatesville, Pennsylvania. I have helped train his media team on the live streaming and audiovisual systems they have installed. The system uses much of what we have talked about in this book and puts it into the context of a real church. Let's start with the live streaming system they have installed and then we can review how they use the projectors and LCD monitors throughout the facility for image magnification.

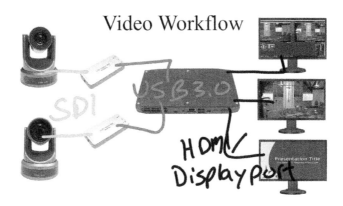

The church decided to use a PTZOptics Producer Kit as their core live streaming and video production system. This system is powered by the superfast Intel NUC Skull Canyon computer. As you can see, the cameras are each connected to an SDI capture card which plugs into the computer via USB 3.0. The computer is connected to three monitors. One monitor is displaying the video production software, one monitor is showing a full-screen camera preview, and the third monitor is dedicated to PowerPoint.

Monitor 1	Monitor 2	Monitor 3
Video Production software	Camera Preview	PowerPoint

We have the monitors laid out in a way that is intuitive for the volunteers that the church relies on every Sunday. To make things easier, they also have a little cheat sheet right next to the joystick controller to show the PTZ presets assigned to each camera. Finally, all of the volunteers know that whatever is displayed on monitor 3 will be going out to the projection and LCD system. Therefore, if they want to switch between the PowerPoint presentation and the live camera feeds they simply need to toggle on or off the "full screen" button inside vMix which is the live streaming software they have selected.

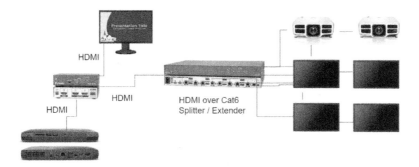

As you can see the Olivet United Methodist Church is using an HDMI distribution system to extend the video from their live streaming computer to two projectors and four television displays located throughout the church. The projectors are used to provide image magnification inside the church. This gives the entire church larger than life views of the pastor and members of the choir. Two of the LCD monitors are used in overflow spaces showing the presentation and live camera feeds in areas that couldn't otherwise see. Two of the LCD monitors are used to give the folks on either side of the stage a better view of the subject material from PowerPoint or the live cameras.

CHURCH
Pro Video Tip

Image magnification is one of the most advanced features requested by churches. Follow the steps we have outlined to troubleshoot any issues you may be having. Do not hesistate to consult with a professional.

Image magnification is often referred to as "IMAG" by church media directors. Media directors can sometimes have control over multiple screens throughout a space where they are making decisions about what content they can display to support the worship atmosphere. Adrian Lopez, the lead director of live production at Gateway Church in Southlake, Texas says "IMAG needs to magnify what's happening on the platform, while broadcast needs more visual context." At many churches, media directors are expected to "provide high-quality video support for overflow areas, digital signage, satellite campuses, live streaming, and on-demand digital delivery" which as you can imagine will take a well-trained team to deliver. Lopez says, "Our IMAG has already been intended as a complement to the worship atmosphere, working side by side with the worship and lighting, all without being distracting" (Schwindt, 2018).

Robb Mactavish, the live production director at the Flatirons Community Church in Lafayette, Colorado says "It's ultimately about creating a modern space where people want to come and experience it, because we want them to bump into Jesus" (Schwindt, 2018). It's worth reviewing the importance of the audiovisual workflow and the overall system design chain when you are considering latency for image magnification. In a church, near-zero latency is important because so much music and in-room focus happens inside the space. It can be distracting for church members to look up at a large projection screen that is showing something happening right in front of them, but one or two seconds behind real-time. Generally, from my experience, I have found that the longer your audiovisual chain of equipment is, the longer your latency will become. Each piece of audiovisual equipment, including your live streaming computer, video extension hardware, cameras, cabling, and other format converters will all add to the overall latency of video delivery. This latency may seem insignificant during the testing of a single piece of hardware but put into a large chain of equipment the latency can become quite apparent.

On a recent installation, I found that using vMix with the included "Low Latency Capture" optimization settings checked "on" can make your video inputs significantly faster. We have also found that there is a BIG difference between free software such as OBS and paid for software such as vMix and Wirecast in these scenarios. Using high-quality video production software and equipment is essential in scenarios where you want to eliminate latency and magnify images for a live audience. If you are trying to troubleshoot an image magnification issue, test by taking pieces of equipment out of the chain one by one. In this way you can minimize the cable path to your final destination.

After just two months of live streaming, Olivet United Methodist Church has enjoyed great success particularly on Facebook. The new live streaming system was in place just before Christmas. In that time, the church media team was able to live stream a candle light service, the Christmas service and a baptism. The live streaming system has connected house bound parishioners like Tori Parker who commented "Glad I can be here, even from my couch as I recover from surgery." The system has also connected members who have moved away from the area like Agnes Miner who says "What a blessing to happen (though I'm not convinced things just "happen") to check my Facebook feed just a few minutes before 10 this morning and discover your first live feed of your service! And then to discover Pastor Spiegelhalder was participating, and the service included the baptism of his great-granddaughter! It's been 40 years since our family lived in Coatesville and were active at Olivet. What a joy to participate in the service remotely!" It's comments like these that remind us why we live stream church services.

10 TIPS FROM FRIENDS AND INDUSTRY EXPERTS

Now it's time to reflect on some tips and tricks given to me by some of my dearest friends and experts in the industry. In this chapter, we will hear from members of our "Churches That Live Stream" Facebook Group including Brooks Willig of San Angelo, Texas, Phil Thompson and Steve Lacy of Oro Valley, Arizona, Jason Jenkins from Everett, Washington, and Christopher M. Chinni. Each of these video production experts has a story to tell and tips that may prove invaluable to you. Let's start with Phil and Steve's emergency checklist.

Phil Thompson & Steve Lacy of StreamingChurch.TV, Oro Valley, AZ

Emergency #1 - Buffering & Skipping

What happens when your video stream starts to buffer and skip? The common issue here is lack of bandwidth. You need to increase your upload speed most likely. In Wirecast, the broadcast icon will change colors from green to yellow or red. In vMix, the stream button will change color from red (which means broadcasting live without issue) to yellow or orange. In OBS, there's a similar alert on the lower right-hand part of the screen showing the stream status.

Next, run a speed test at speedof.me to measure your current upload speed. Remember we are looking for upload speed, not download speeds. As a rule, you should have twice the amount of upload speed as you are consuming with your stream.

720p can be between 1.5-4Mbps.

1080p can be between 2-6Mbps.

4K can be between 8-30Mbps.

Another option is purchasing a dedicated ISP service for your broadcast PC.

Emergency #2 - Pixilation

Pixilation is normally due to your encoder not being able to encode your stream fast enough. Commonly, the

CHURCH
Pro Video Tip

In Windows, you can open up the Task Manager using CONTROL + ALT + DELETE . You can use the performance table to view your computers CPU and GPU usage. Always try to use your GPU whenever possible.

moving parts of the video image are pixelated while the static items remain crisp. The encoder works hardest when the video contains moving subjects and backgrounds. Encoding your stream can be very taxing on your computer. You'll want to make sure that the CPU on your computer doesn't reach above 80% at any time you're streaming.

Option 1: Reduce the workload of your computer.

Option 2: Upgrade your computer.

To reduce the workload on your computer, you can change your encoder settings to either remove some additional streams and change the settings of your existing streams. Removing one of your two streams can reduce the CPU load by almost 50%. The key parameters to reduce the workload when encoding a single stream include the stream resolution, the stream bit rate, and the stream frame rate. Changing your frame rate from 60 frames per second to 30 frames per second can reduce the encoder workload by 50%. So, set your frames per second at 30 frames per second. Reducing your broadcast speed and resolution can also dramatically reduce the workload on your encoder although certain resolutions require minimum broadcast bit rates to broadcast properly.

Emergency #3 - Unable to stream

If your encoder is unable to connect, the first thing to test is that you have a good internet connection on the encoder computer. Launch a web browser on the encoder computer and navigate to a known website. If you have a good internet connection, the likely problem is your stream key.

Try to copy and paste your stream keys into your encoder software once more. If this doesn't work, try refreshing the keys from YouTube/Facebook or another CDN.

Emergency #4 - No audio

The first thing to check is the audio output level/setting on your encoder. Make sure the audio setting is appropriate. If you've had audio in weeks prior and you don't have any audio now, then you should first check for loose or disconnected audio cables to the encoding computer. If the cables check out OK, then check to see if the audio source is sending audio to your encoding computer. A common problem is the sound guy may have muted the audio feed to the live stream. If you still haven't found the issue, then it's time to double check your encoder audio settings to ensure you've selected the proper audio source. If you still haven't found the issue, then it might be time to test the audio input using a pair of headphones to determine where the audio outage is occurring.

On CPU load for live streaming computers

To get an accurate idea of how your processor is doing, you will need to have everything up and running including your live encoder as you stream. If your computer is running above 70% CPU, I would be a little nervous. If its above 80%, I would be nervous. If it's above 90%, I would leave the room and run for the hills. Just kidding about that one, but anytime your CPU runs over 70 to 80%, it's going to cause problems with your streaming video. Video buffering, video pixilation, and more problems will develop. If your CPU runs high, you need to examine the resolution that you are streaming. You may need to lower it. If you are sending multiple streams, that can be taxing on your computer. If you are recording your service using your live encoder that can drain your computer's resources. One solution is to beef up your computer's processor and ram.

TIP: You can also use restreaming services now available in the cloud. Check out restream.io and switchboard.live. These services will take a single live stream and restream them out to multiple destinations for you in the cloud. This will reduce your overall bandwidth and computer processing requirements.

Jason Jenkins from the DVeStore

#1 What do you want to accomplish?

1. We want to increase the production value of our services by sending live video and graphics to multiple screens.
2. We want to live stream our church services, to increase our audience and spread the good word!
3. We want to record our sermons, and upload them to Vimeo or YouTube, so that our house-bound parishioners can watch them at home.

#2 How many cameras do you want? Will you have camera operators?

A church just starting out may only need a single camera. Others may want three to five, or more… If they don't have employees or volunteers to operate these cameras, the conversation turns to PTZ cameras (Pan, Tilt and Zoom).

You may want to consider the scalability of your system. Can you easily add cameras in the future? Can you easily add additional video inputs or outputs in the future?

#3 How is your Audio?

You can have the greatest video in the world, and bad audio will make the entire stream a wasted effort. It could be that a simple microphone upgrade can significantly improve your audio results. You may need a more powerful microphone transmitter to counteract signal loss.

#4 How is your lighting?

Any camera can benefit from good lighting. A common problem is not enough light. Without enough light, the cameras will compensate with a larger aperture and additional gain which will increase the image noise.

Another frequent issue is that of mixed color temperatures. If you have tungsten lighting in your chapel, plus natural light from windows, you have a *Clash of the Kelvins*! You can either invest in drapes/shades to block out daylight or replace interior lights with daylight fixtures to color match each.

#5 What equipment do you have now and what new equipment will be integrated?

Appliance Switchers
- Roland
- TriCaster
- BlackMagic ATEM
- Livestream
- Wirecast Gear

Software Switchers
- vMix (PC only)
- mimoLive (Mac only)
- BlackMagic ATEM (PC/Mac)
- Wirecast (PC/Mac)
- Livestream Studio (PC/Mac)

Setting Realistic Expectations with Christopher M. Chinni

Dos:

Do plan for your first months' worth of streaming services to have issues.

Do try to have someone you trust watch from outside your churches network. Either using cellular data or from home. Allow them to provide you live feedback via text.

CHURCH
Pro Video Tip

YouTube has a great feature called "unlisted" video streaming. You can set your live stream to be unlisted and only the people you share the link with will be able to see it.

Don'ts:

Don't expect perfection without practice. And it's hard to practice without a "live" service.

Don't be discouraged by a small audience. Everyone attending online is someone who would not be in service otherwise.

Don't look at your streaming statistics on a regular basis. Statistics and metrics are for businesses; you are using the internet to perform the Great Commission. There are no number requirements in that verse. ☐ –

Brooks Willig, Western Audio Works, San Angelo, TX

If you have multiple cameras, I find it better to frame the camera shot off-air and then switch to the camera. Then move the off-air camera to the next shot and switch. PTZ cameras are great solutions for churches that don't have much room to put in camera platforms or operators. They are great for churches with limited staff since one person could frame the camera shots and switch all from one small console.

We mounted a camera close to eye level with someone standing at the pulpit. This angle is best for live IMAG (Image Magnification) shots. If it was at a higher angle like on a ceiling, it could have this looking down from heaven kind of feel. This is great for when you want to show the crowd or people in a room but not so great when you need to watch the preacher on stage for a long time.

11 TUNING YOUR AUDIO-VISUAL SYSTEM

It's time to review how you can tune your audio and video gear inside the church for optimal performance. Many times, churches have amazing lighting and beautifully colored stained glass. It's also common for churches to have lots of hard surfaces and challenging acoustics. When you start to build out an audio-visual system with multiple cameras and microphones, you need to make sure that each camera matches the entire set and your audio mix for each input is well balanced. Let's start by reviewing some camera basics and then we will dig into a high-level overview of audio mixing.

Video Cameras

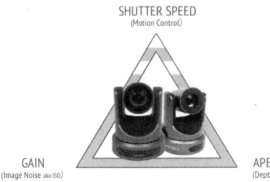

SHUTTER SPEED
(Motion Control)

GAIN
(Image Noise aka ISO)

APERTURE
(Depth of Field)

The first place we want to start with any camera is exposure. In order to get the perfect camera exposure, we need to work with a few core camera settings which include Iris, Shutter Speed, and Gain. Ideally, we want to keep gain (also known as ISO) as low as possible. Start by setting up the cameras in your space with the lighting you plan to use turned on. Try your best to perform your testing during the same time of day that you plan to live stream and record your video at. Churches often have a lot of natural daylight that could significantly alter your manual settings if you set up everything in the evening. Start by referencing the 180-degree shutter speed rule which says that your shutter speed should be double the frame rate that you are recording or broadcasting in.

Understand the 180 Degree Shutter Speed Angle Rule:

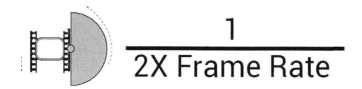

$$\frac{1}{2X \text{ Frame Rate}}$$

For example, if you are live streaming in 1080p @ 30 frames per second then your shutter speed should be set to 1/60. The 180-degree shutter speed rule helps to keep your video looking realistic and smooth to viewers. If your shutter speed is too fast than your video starts to look artificial and object movement looks too crisp and overly detailed. Humans are used to seeing a certain amount of blur when we see an object move quickly in front of our eyes. I highly suggest setting up all your cameras in manual mode when you are tuning your camera's exposure. In this way, you can lock your camera's shutter speed and adjust the iris until you capture the ideal exposure.

The iris of your camera is the opening of the lens which lets a controlled amount of light shine on your camera's sensor. The aperture, also known as the f/stop, controls the opening of the iris. A large aperture (small f/stop number), will create a shallow depth of field. A small aperture (large f/stop number), will create a large depth of field where everything in view is in focus. For recording and streaming live video, our most important goal is to make sure the video looks realistic. With a slow shutter speed that is too slow, objects on camera will look blurry as they move. With a shutter speed that is too fast, moving objects will look un-realistic.

Depending on the lighting available in your church many cameras offer additional features for enhancing the quality of your image. To get the most out of your camera's sensor you will want to create the ideal exposure erroring on the side of slighting under exposed versus over exposed. Photographers call this technique creating a "flat" image because an over exposed image will lose some details as the black and whites are crushed before the image reaches its final destination. For a photographer the "final destination" is generally a photo editing software such as Photoshop. For a live video production, the "final destination" is your video production software and the CDN you are streaming to. If you can create the perfect exposure with a slightly flat image, you can enhance the overall video quality in your video production software using color correction tools to create the best possible live video feed.

You should have a good quality picture coming into your live streaming software before you start tweaking additional camera settings such as contrast, luminance, gamma and hue. Once you have your exposure set properly, it's time to set the cameras white balance. Some cameras support an auto-white balance option which allows the operator to zoom into a white sheet of paper and press a button that adjusts the camera's white balance automatically. Some cameras, like the PTZOptics cameras, support color balancing based on the Kelvin scale which is a scale of color temperatures used in modern lighting. Many churches have older tungsten lighting which puts off a very yellow 3000-3400 Kelvin color light. Other churches have plenty of daylight which is more in the 5500-6500 Kelvin range.

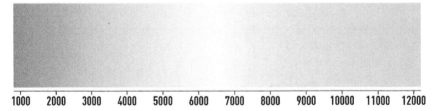

Once your white balance is set properly, many professionals will use a color checker card which is a physical card with every color of the rainbow displayed. You can zoom your cameras into this card to cross reference each video feed and make sure every camera is representing each color identically. Here is a step by step guide for tuning your cameras:

1. Set up your lighting. Light the room or subject you plan to use.
2. Set the exposure of your cameras to a slightly underexposed flat image.
3. Use a white balance card to make sure your white balance is set up properly Adjust your white balance to get a perfect scale of whites to blacks.
4. Now use a color checker card to make sure your camera's color are being displayed accurately
5. Use your video production software tools for color correction and final tuning.

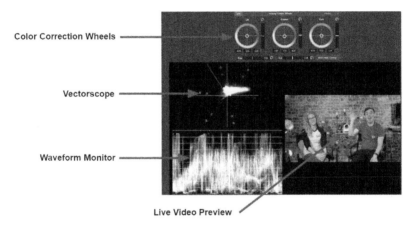

Color Correction Wheels

Vectorscope

Waveform Monitor

Live Video Preview

One of the key mistakes with color correction is trying to make all the adjustments inside the camera. Many times, the highlights can be blown out before they even get into your video production software. Using a vector scope and waveform monitor can help you see exactly what you are working with. Looking at professional tools like this can help you bring down the range of your camera to make sure that you are not clipping your sensors capabilities. These tools make sure that you are not crushing the blacks or overexposing the whites with the settings in your camera. The waveform monitor specifically allows users to stretch the exposure to the perfect white and black settings.

A vector scope is a tool that represents the color of your camera's image. It's an x and y graph that represents the color accuracy of your live video feed. At the top of a vector scope you have red, toward the bottom you have cyan and there is also a green like what you may have seen in color correction software. The vector scope graph allows you to see the balance of colors coming from your live video camera. To accurately tune your camera, you can put up a color chart in your space and zoom into it with your camera.

The waveform monitor is the counterpart of the vector scope used to handle brightness and exposure. With a waveform monitor, you can easily see if your image is clipping at the top or if the blacks are getting crushed. The waveform monitor will allow camera operators the ability to adjust the image preferably in the camera first to ensure your image has a good exposure. Using the waveform monitor to influence your camera settings adjustments, you want your camera's image to be within the range of your monitor.

It's a wise idea to purchase good quality monitors for your video production team. Trying to color match multiple cameras with a low-quality monitor is an impossible task. Using tools like the waveform monitor and vector scope will make the job easier. Do yourself a favor and purchase at least one good quality video monitor.

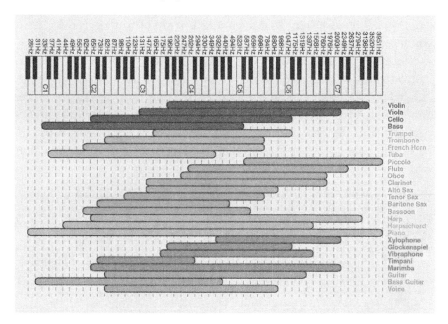

Now let's start our high-level conversation about mixing audio by looking at a frequency range chart above. This chart includes all the instruments of an orchestra next to the human voice. Audio is measured in hertz which is the "derived unit of frequency in the International System of Units (SI) and is defined as one cycle per second" (Wikipedia, 2019). I know this sounds incredibly complicated but essentially each instrument above will produce audio in the ranges shown on the chart above (Netcom, 2019). As you can see, understanding the difference between each instrument and how they should sound in your church's audio mixing board should be considered a high art. In this book, we are simply going to review some high levels suggestions to improve your church's audio mix and refer you to an amazing book by Dr. Barry R. Hill called "Mixing for God". Mixing for God is the best book I have found on the subject which truly is a "Volunteer's Guide to Church Sound."

As you create the audio mix for your church's sound, you want to listen to each instrument individually. Don't make the mistake of only listening to the instruments through your audio mixer. The job of an audio engineer is to understand what each instrument sounds like in real life and then tune the audio board appropriately. You should ask performers to play their instruments for you so that you can listen for sonic qualities. It's a great idea to ask each instrumentalist and singer to play a scale for you so that you can get an idea of what they sound like in the space without the microphones and audio mixer. Don't be afraid to ask questions. Maybe you can ask performers if they have a specific microphone they like to use. Some performers may even have experience using an EQ and they can give you advice on which frequencies to cut in their input.

Once you have a good idea of what each instrument should sound like cataloged in your brain, you are ready to move over to the mixing board. Now you will want to use the "solo" feature of the mixing board to listen to each instrumentalist individually through your audio mixer. Make sure that you have high quality headphones that allow you to hear each instrument and the entire mix when you need to without distraction (don't use ear buds). A well-trained audio engineer should be able to pick out each instrument just by listening to the entire mix. But if you are just getting started, try using the solo button to hone in on one instrument at a time. A great tip for volunteers interested in audio production is pick out a favorite DAW (Digital Audio Workstation) software and create recordings that you can take home with you. If you take home a 16-channel multi-track audio recording, you can spend time during the week, creating a mix that you can bring back to church the following Sunday.

Once you have listened to each instrument individually it's time to create an overall audio mix. Looking at a chart that helps you reference each individual instrument frequency ranges will help you equalize each input. Simply knowing that the human voice has a range of 80 Hz- 8,000 Hz can help you significantly when you are mixing your audio. If you have a singer's microphone picking up frequencies above 8,000 Hz you can bet that they are not coming from the singer's voice. If you are picking up low end frequencies below 80 Hz then you know they are also coming something other than the singer's voice.

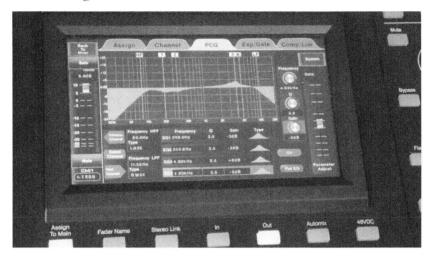

The picture above shows a parametric equalizer used to equalize the voice of a singer. After listening to the singer and knowing that human voice cannot go below 80 Hz a high-pass (same as a low-cut) filter, can be applied starting at roughly 80 Hz. On the other end of the spectrum you can see a low-pass (same as a high-cut) filter used to remove noise on the high end of the frequency spectrum. Using simple high and low pass filters are a great place to start cleaning up your audio mix.

Audio Description	Frequency Range
SHEEN	12 kHz to 16 kHz
SIBILANCE	5 kHz to 8 kHz
PRESENCE	3 kHz to 5 kHz
VOCAL CLARITY	800 to 2000 Hz
NASAL VOICE	400 to 600 Hz
FULLNESS VOICE	200 to 400 Hz
BOOM	80 to 200 Hz
DEEP BASS	30 to 80 Hz

Once you have cleaned up the audio with filters, it's time to enhance the audio's "texture" with the EQ. Often, I find that churches have the audio mixer EQ knobs adjusted to what seems like random positions. Start by setting all your frequency knobs back to the 12 o'clock position. From here you can start to enhance the sound of each instrument. You may find it helpful to put words to each category of your audio mixers equalization section. Using these words can help you try to visualize the way you are sculpting each input with your EQ.

There is so much more to learn about audio mixing. If you have the passion to learn about audio mixing on behalf of your church I highly recommend reading, *Mixing for God* by Dr. Barry Hill. Dr. Barry R. Hill is professor of music and director of the Audio & Music Production degree program at Lebanon Valley College in Pennsylvania. One of his students now works with our team helping us tune our audio systems both in studio and on site when we setup live video productions.

12 THE DIGITAL PASTOR & ONLINE CONTRIBUTORS

Attracting new members is a top priority for most churches. So, how will live streaming your church services online help attract new members? If our church services are available online, won't people just watch from home?

I think that Seth Haberman, better known as the "Digital Pastor" put it best when he sarcastically said "Ever since Grace Church started live streaming... I don't have to go to church anymore. I can stay home and literally just watch church from my chair... and I don't have to go through that stupid greeting... go and find three people and give them a fist bump. How about I give myself a fist bump?" (Haberman, 2017).

The Basics of Church Live Streaming
131,081 views

I love the context that Seth Haberman jokingly brings into the introduction to his video "The Basics of Church Streaming". For good reason, many churches have been worried whether live streaming will keep members from coming into the church. Is it possible that your church's current members will stay home instead of attending church in person? Yes. This is a question almost every church brings up when they start to think about live streaming.

These were legitimate concerns in the infancy stages of live streaming adoption only three to five years ago. Ever since social media websites such as YouTube and Facebook have started to allow organizations to live stream their original content for free, churches have been scrambling to figure out this new technology. Could live streaming be used to spread the message of God? Will our online viewers feel compelled to come into the church?

"Live streaming has recently become popular... super popular... not only in the church but also on social media" Haberman explains. "Live streaming can be an incredibly powerful tool for the use of the church. Churches can now reach people outside the four walls of their church in a way never before possible." Haberman goes on to explain that "you don't need a half a million dollar budget anymore to start live streaming" and "through live streaming, your church can reach people that are not Christian... maybe someone who is intimidated or nervous about coming into your church or church members who are simply out of town on vacation... they could be elderly members who cannot physically make it into church, or they could even be people who are looking for a church online that have come across a link to your live stream" (Haberman, 2017).

Seth Haberman is a friend of mine, who I have spoken with at great length about churches using live streaming to enhance their outreach capabilities. We both agree that the number one reason churches fail to start live streaming is out of fear. Many churches are afraid that current members may stay at home and watch the services online instead of attending in person. While this is a possibility, almost every church I have spoken to about this says that its live video program brings people into the church. "In my experience, this has not been an issue with churches I have worked with," says Haberman (Haberman, 2017).

When we are considering the power of live streaming, we are also talking about the massive reach of social media. With the right strategy put into place, your live videos can turn online viewers into lifelong supporters of the church. New technologies are allowing churches to accept digital donations both through their websites and social media pages directly. Your influence online can now become a bridge for new members giving them the nudge of confidence they need to walk through your church's front doors. We all must remember that watching a church service online will always pale in comparison to the real thing. The ultimate value of a church service comes from an authentic experience with God, and the community inside your church enhances those moments in a way that cannot be replicated inside an online chatroom.

CHURCH
Pro Video Tip

Putting a digital donation service in place will be a critical step in growing your churches online presence. Make sure to include information about how folks can give online inside your live stream.

While live streaming experiences like these may transcend the barriers of your church's four walls, the heartbeat of your community will always be inside your church's brick and mortar location. To be clearer, I believe that your church services may have a profound impact on viewers around the world. These viewers may or may not be Christians. These viewers may have spent years looking for faith in all the wrong places. With the right strategy, your online video content should have the ability to help people realize what they are missing each Sunday and prompt them to take the next logical step toward becoming closer to God and your church.

Let's assume that the goal for your live streaming program is growing your community, accepting new members, and spreading the message of God. Accepting contributions online may become a major revenue stream to help support and grow your church. Most churches that I have worked with prefer the term "digital contributions" over "digital donations." The words "contribution" and "contributor" generally hold higher esteem than "donations" and "donor."

There are multiple ways to get started accepting online contributions. Perhaps the easiest way to get started is to put a button on your website. Most churches will use a PayPal account to set up a contribution button on their website, but I highly recommend Pushpay.com as well. Having a digital donation service dedicated to worship giving can have a transformational effect on your church's fundraising capabilities. Once your donation account is all set up, you can have a simple button put on your website by copying and pasting the custom HTML code into your website editor. This button will allow your members to make financial contributions directly to your PayPal or Pushpay account. You can then transfer the funds directly to your bank account. Think about all the time you could be saving every week!

Services such as Pushpay and Tithe.ly make it easier for churches to set up recurring giving. Pushpay says "Recurring givers are the lifeblood of every church. Not only do these donors give 42% more annually than one-time donors but they also help churches maintain a steady budget during the ups and downs of giving throughout the year." Digital giving services can help increase giving overall with online tools that include mobile giving, text giving, and membership giving management. Steve Murray, the Pastor of Real Life Church, says "Sunday morning is no longer the main place that people give. We are starting to see people giving while they are on vacation and giving on a Sunday that they are not at church. People can give directly from their seat before the buckets even get around. Young people have even started to give" (PushPay, 2018).

Kevin Johnson of the Dare to Imagine Church, in Philadelphia, Pennsylvania said "We had this blizzard that came out of nowhere that just wrecked the entire east coast. Initially, we were a little concerned with what we were going to do. So, we had worship via a conference call and I'm happy to say that we did what we normally do on a regular Sunday. We couldn't have done that just one year ago." PushPay estimates that a church with 200 members that generally raises $250,000 per year can increase annual giving by roughly $20,000. This can come from new first-time giving, new recurring giving migrated cash-and-check givers, and the reduction of lost donations (PushPay, 2018).

It's a good idea to put a digital contribution button right next to your live video stream on your website. You can now accept digital donations directly through major social media such as Facebook and YouTube, which I believe may be **the #1 way churches can increase first time giving**. Many churches embed their YouTube live stream video players on a specific page of their website. But at the same time, the live stream will also get distributed on social media networks automatically by default. I suggest putting your in-house digital donation button right next to the live video on your website with a short explanation of the church. At the same time, you will likely find that Facebook and YouTube are generating online donations for you as well. Starting in 2018, Facebook and YouTube both started making it easier for non-profit organizations to accept donations directly through their social media pages during live streams. These new features are powerful, easy to use, and incredibly scalable.

Let's start with accepting contributions on Facebook. The first thing you will need to do is make sure that your church is registered with the IRS (Internal Revenue Service) as an authorized 501(c)(3) non-profit organization. You can find the official application process here (https://www.irs.gov/charities-non-profits). Once your church is officially recognized as a 501(c)(3) you can set up your Facebook page as a "not for profit" in the category area of your page settings.

Once Facebook approves your new page status, every time your page gets mentioned on Facebook, users will be prompted with a question about whether they would like to include a donation button for your organization as part of their post. This process is so intuitive and wide-reaching my team was able to raise $90 for a local non-profit in West Chester, Pennsylvania by accident! We were live streaming a local fashion show where the Family Lives On Foundation was involved. Simply because we "tagged" this organization in our Facebook live stream post, it prompted us to include a donation button. We raised $90 for this charity without even planning on it!

Armed with this knowledge you can empower organizations that want to support you by collecting donations online on your behalf. You can also include a convenient button for your viewers to donate with directly inside the Facebook platform. Facebook does a fantastic job collecting donations, potentially sharing your events with connected networks which can promote others to join in on the giving. For example, when you donate, you can select whether others will be able to see your donation in the stream chatroom. You can also request that your donation remain private as well.

Facebook says this about fundraising on the platform "Before making your ask, build a strong Facebook presence. You'll want to post 2-3 times per week to tell your organization's story and the impact you've had. When you're ready to make your appeal to donors, do so in a thoughtful way. When you post, include a call to action that makes it clear what you're asking for and what your organization's priorities are." If you are live streaming your Sunday services, this is the perfect place to deliver your value and make a compelling pitch (Facebook, 2016).

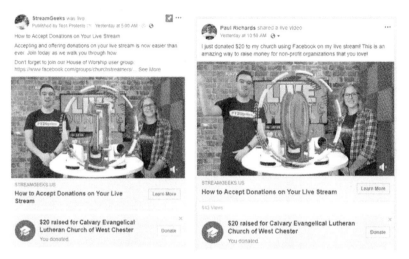

YouTube offers a similar feature called "Super Chat." Super Chats are highlighted messages inside the YouTube Live chatroom that include a monetary contribution to your organization. Again, your organization will have to be registered as a 501(c)(3) non-profit with Google to accept tax-free donations. Once you are all set up, other YouTube channels can elect to send donations from their channels to live stream directly to your organization as well. This is a great way to enable other organizations to sponsor your church and accept donations on your behalf. Does someone in your church have a large following on YouTube? Do you have an event that might attract a large audience? These are perfect opportunities to raise funds on social media.

Note: YouTube is currently in the process of implementing a new feature called **Super Chats for Good**. Currently, YouTube requires channels to have 1,000 subscribers to use the Super Chat feature. Super Chat for Good allows any channel with Super Chat enabled to direct funds to a charity of the owner's choice. 100% of all donations are given to the charity selected (YouTube Help, 2018).

How to Accept Donations on Your LIVE Stream

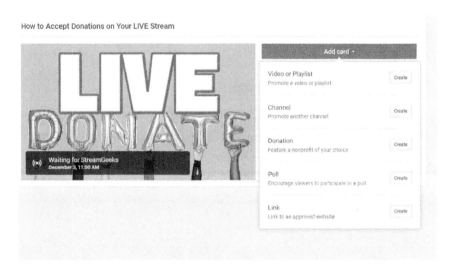

Another great way to start accepting donations through YouTube is through a feature called cards. Cards show up in the top right portion of your video as a little circle with an "i" which stands for more "information." These cards can include information about where the donation is going, and you can select any 501(c)(3) non-profit in Google's registered database. This is a great feature to include in all of your YouTube live streams and videos. You can add cards to your existing live streams and video using the YouTube video editor in the creator studio.

As you can see, connecting your church on social media can significantly increase the number of online contributions your church can receive. It will also make your church more visible to outside organizations that want to help. Getting your social media accounts up and running will make it easier for others to make contributions to your organization.

To get the most out of these tools, a little strategy can go a long way. Taking a moment to explain the tools you are using to your church members and your online audience will have a huge impact on the effectiveness of your fundraising. When it comes time for collections at your church, simply mentioning that there is an online contribution option should suggest to your live stream viewers that they can donate online. Making it a part of your regular routine should pay dividends in the future. Remember to mention the new tools you are using, and your digital contributions will flourish. Acknowledging your online audience's requests for prayers and other comments can also go a long way.

13 THE BASICS OF IP NETWORKING

The purpose of this chapter will be to provide a basic understanding of how IP networks are set up as it applies to video production. To help churches start at a crawl and eventually make it to a run, we will be focusing on the NewTek NDI (Network Device Interface) IP video production standard mentioned throughout this book. NDI is a paradigm shift that will increase what is possible in all things live video. In this chapter, we will think outside the box about how to plan out live streaming and video production systems in the world of IP. Using standard networking infrastructure, NDI will enable you to do more with less. Together we will uncover new possibilities for low budget streaming and high-end video production systems alike as we move toward the future of broadcast video over IP. If you want to get started testing out NDI right away, you can download a free set of NDI tools at newtek.com/ndi/tools.

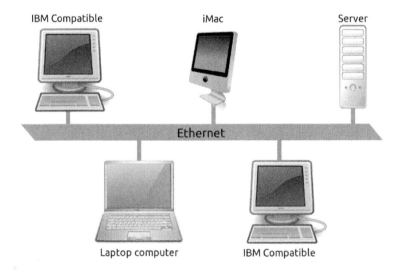

Let's talk about the basics. Ethernet cables connect each device to a network switch which acts like a hub inside your LAN (Local Area Network). A local area network is a group of computers and associated devices that share communications lines or wireless links to a server or router. Every device you have on your network has an IP address which Wikipedia calls "An **Internet Protocol address**... a numerical label assigned to each device" (Wikipedia, 2019). An IP address generally looks like this **191.168.1.100** but it could also look like this **216.3.128.12**.

Let's look at an example IP address table. It's important that you are organized when it comes to managing the 254 IP addresses available on a single IP range.

IP Address	Device
192.168.1.0	This is the network number that identifies the network as a whole
192.168.1.1	This is assigned to the router
192.168.1.2-254	These addresses may be assigned to devices on your network
192.168.1.255	This is the broadcast address. Anything sent to this address is automatically broadcast to IP addresses 1-254

Now let's look at an example church network. For this example, we will segment out several parts of the network for devices that are used for video production such as cameras and computers powering displays. There are two different ways that we can assign devices IP addresses. They can be assigned a static IP address manually or a dynamic IP address automatically. Static IP addresses never change, and therefore they are much better for managing an IP address table on your network. Dynamic IP addresses are assigned by your router using DHCP (Dynamic Host Configuration Protocol). DHCP is ideal for devices that periodically connect and disconnect from your network. A prime example of an IP connected device that uses DHCP is a smartphone. When your smartphone connects to WiFi, it automatically gets an IP address from the network. It's considered best practice to assign static IP addresses to the most important devices on your network used for video production. It's especially important to use a static IP address for devices like cameras that communicate directly with your video production software using the address.

Without getting too complicated into networking jargon, you can have up to 254 devices on a single network which can all communicate on the same IP range. The network above as a whole are defined as 192.168.1.0 and the router would usually be assigned the very first address as 192.168.1.1. Your router is usually given to you by your ISP (Internet Service Provider), and this device may include a built-in network switch, a firewall, and a built-in Wi-Fi access point. Therefore, many routers today will allow you to connect devices to your network right away such as a smart TV, your smartphone, and perhaps a few computers. For video production, you will likely want to purchase a dedicated network switch which will allow you to plug multiple devices into your network. Your network switch is connected to your router with an ethernet cable. Remember that ethernet cables can become a bottleneck in your bandwidth access and we will always be selecting ethernet cables that match our networking infrastructures bandwidth capabilities. If you are planning to power your cameras using ethernet cables, you will want to make sure to purchase a network switch that supports PoE (Power Over Ethernet).

IP Address	Device
192.168.1.0	Network Address
192.168.1.1	Router supplied by your Internet Service Provider
192.168.1.2-59	Used for office devices like office computers, printers, access points, and other IP connected devices
192.168.1.60	PTZOptics 20X - Main Camera in back of Church
192.168.1.61	PTZOptics 12X - Front Camera on Choir Area

192.168.1.62	PTZOptics 12X - Side Camera to on Stage
192.168.1.63	PTZOptics 30X - 2nd Camera in back of Church for Close Up Views
192.168.1.64	PTZOptics ZCam - Static Camera used for Drum Cage
192.168.1.65	PTZOptics ZCam - Static Camera used for Backstage
192.168.1.66	PTZOptics IP Joystick Controller
192.168.1.70	Main Live Streaming Computer
192.168.1.71	Pastor's on-Stage Laptop
192.168.1.72	Computer Powering 2 Displays in Lobby using NDI Studio Monitor
192.168.1.73	Computer Powering 2 Displays in Nursery using NDI Studio Monitor
192.168.1.74	Computer Powering 2 Displays on Stage for Confidence Monitoring
192.168.1.119*	iPad using NDI Camera App (Wireless Camera)
192.168.1.123*	Smartphone used for iOS camera control app
*Assigned with DHCP	

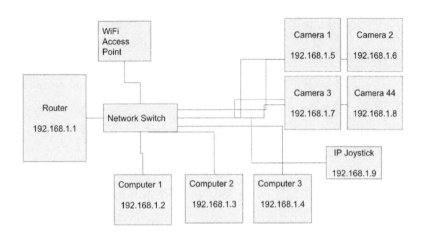

The great thing about IP based video production for so many churches is that you already have a network in place. If you have internet at home, then you may even have a home network that may make more sense to you by looking at the above diagram. You can open up a whole new universe of possibilities, where the network you already have has become the preferred method of video routing across your facility. Need another camera shot? Just run a single Cat-5e cable to an NDI camera, and you will have high-quality video, a camera you can remotely control, and power for that camera solved in a single stroke Want to send PowerPoint slides from the pastor's computer on stage back to the video production computer? No problem, everything is connected to the same network.

This is where the rubber meets the road. Unlike SDI and HDMI cabling, ethernet can provide power for cameras using a PoE source, such as a PoE switch. It will simplify installations and eliminate the need for additional outlets where you would have had to hire an electrician in the past. And unlike traditional RS-223 camera control cables, ethernet can also be used to control cameras and devices within your favorite video production software. You can even use an IP joystick without requiring direct analog control cabling to each camera like before. This technology is such a game changer I have asked PoE Texas CEO, Tyler Andrews to write an introductory overview in the next chapter.

PRODUCTION STUDIO

Now let's review the bandwidth available on your network infrastructure to be used for IP based video distribution. Just like the category cabling we mentioned early, networking equipment has bandwidth limitations. Most commonly installed networking equipment has a bandwidth limit of either 10/100 or gigabit. Unfortunately, if you have 10/100 networking infrastructure, you cannot use it for IP based video production. There isn't enough bandwidth on these older networking systems to support video transmission. The good news is that gigabit networking equipment has become the industry standard and there is a good chance this is the type of technology you already have installed. A gigabit network switch with a full throughput backplane can send approximately 1,000 megabits of data to each device on your network. You should never use 100% of the available bandwidth on your network because you need to reserve "headroom" to avoid network congestion and failure. Network bandwidth headroom recommendations can vary widely but generally; most IT professionals recommend 30% - 60% depending on what the network is utilized for. You should consider consulting your network administrator before adding IP video traffic on to your local area network. NewTek suggests "NDI traffic should not take up more than 75% of the bandwidth of any network link" (NewTek, 2016).

There are many different types of network switches that can support various levels of bandwidth. While gigabit is the most popular, today you can purchase 10-gigabit ethernet switches that provide 10,000 megabits per second of transfer speeds. As time moves forward, access to higher bandwidth devices will become more and more common. It's incredible how far we have come already, and things are moving faster than ever before.

Now let's take a moment to understand the bandwidth options we have, so that we can optimize our network for the video sources we want to use. Since we are using the NewTek NDI as our example IP video production solution, let's review at the two main types of NDI video: NDI and NDI HX. NDI is considered the full bandwidth compression version which can take a 3 gigabit, fully uncompressed video signal, and compress it down to 125-200 megabits without producing noticeable digital artifacts. This type of compression is what makes IP video production possible on a gigabit network infrastructure. The compressions effect is "un-noticeable" to the human eye and completely un-noticeable once the video reaches its destination. Since the destination for much of our live video sources is a content delivery network like Facebook and YouTube, we know that the video is going to be compressed anyway with h.264 via RTMP before it reaches our end viewers. The compression technology today is good that the benefits of uncompressed video are only reserved for the highest end television video production studios and Hollywood producers.

To further advance what is possible with IP based video production, NewTek released a "High Efficiency" version of NDI called "NDI HX". This version of NDI can compress a 1080p video source down to mere 8-20 Mbps depending on the selected quality. NDI HX is available in compression ratios of low, medium and high. Let's look at the differences in bandwidth using the chart below.

NDI Mode	Bandwidth
HDI|HX Low (720p60fps)	6 Mbps
NDI|HX Medium (1080p30fps)	8 Mbps
NDI|HX High (1080p60fps)	12 Mbps
NDI (1080p30-60fps)	125-200 Mbps (Nominal Range)

As you can see, there is a big difference between using "full NDI" and NDI HX sources on your network. If you plan on using a lot of NDI sources on your gigabit network switch and respecting the recommended 30-60% headroom space for reliability, your available bandwidth can quickly get used up. Let's look at an example bandwidth consumption table below.

Example:

NDI Device Examples (1080p60fps)	Bandwidth	Accumulated Bandwidth	Total % of Gigabit Network Switch
NDI Scan Converter on Laptop for PowerPoint slides	125 Mbps	125 Mbps	12.5%
2 x NDI Monitor for camera operators	125 Mbps / Each	375 Mbps	12.5% / Each
vMix System	125 Mbps	500 Mbps	12.5%

output in 1080p60fps			
NDI Monitor in Overflow Room	125 Mbps	625 Mbps	12.5%
5 x PTZOptics NDI|HX (High)	12 Mbps / Each	685 Mbps	1.2% / Each
Suggested Headroom	250 Mbps	910 Mbps	25%
Total Usage			**91%**

Multiple types of IP video streaming are used in video production today. The most common of these IP streaming types are RTSP, RTMP, and NDI. Let's talk a little bit about RTSP and RTMP. RTSP stands for real-time streaming protocol, and it is a widely used protocol for streaming video and audio on your local area network. RTSP if perfect for viewing a live camera that is available on your local area network. RTMP stands for real-time messaging protocol and it used by CDNs such as YouTube and Facebook for streaming your live production over the public internet. It's important to think about the differences between IP video that is on your LAN (Local Area Network) and video that sent over the WAN (Wide Area Network). I have included the following diagram below to help illustrate this process.

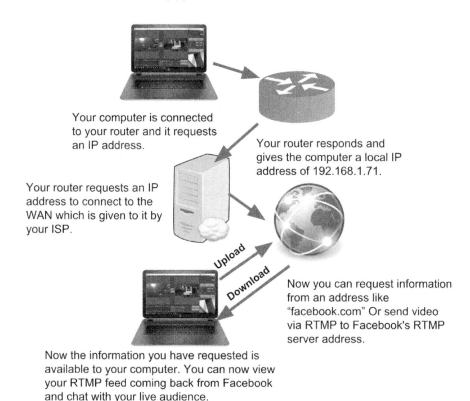

Your computer is connected to your router and it requests an IP address.

Your router responds and gives the computer a local IP address of 192.168.1.71.

Your router requests an IP address to connect to the WAN which is given to it by your ISP.

Now you can request information from an address like "facebook.com" Or send video via RTMP to Facebook's RTMP server address.

Now the information you have requested is available to your computer. You can now view your RTMP feed coming back from Facebook and chat with your live audience.

Now it's time to talk about multicast network traffic. This is as advanced as we will get in this book when it comes to network traffic. But this is an incredibly important technology to understand when it comes to IP based video production. Multicast is a method of sending data to multiple computers on your LAN without incurring additional bandwidth for each receiver. Multicast is very different from unicast which is a data transport method that opens up a unique stream of data between each sender and receiver. Multicast allows you to broadcast video from a single camera or live streaming computer to multiple destinations inside your church without accumulating additional bandwidth on your network for each receiving device. Churches are using multicast to have a camera operator on one computer viewing the video feed and the live streaming computer using the same feed at the same time.

Funny enough, this is a technology that many of us have at home built into our television receiver boxes. When you request an on-demand video from your cable television provider, this opens up a unicast stream for that unique video. When you are flipping through the hundreds of available television channels, this is using multicast. This is how your cable television provider can send thousands of video channels to your television using the same ethernet cabling your church can use.

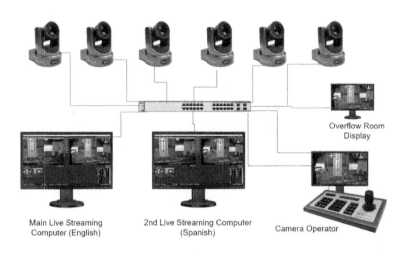

Main Live Streaming Computer (English)
2nd Live Streaming Computer (Spanish)
Camera Operator
Overflow Room Display

MODEL	AREA	POE	IP ADDRESS	MULTICAST ADDRESS
PT20X-NDI-GY	CHURCH FRONT	Y	192.168.100.31	234.1.0.31
PT20X-SDI-GY-G2	CHURCH FRONT	Y	192.168.100.32	234.1.0.32
PT20X-SDI-WH-G2	CHURCH FRONT	Y	192.168.100.33	234.1.0.33
PT20X-SDI-WH-G2	CHURCH FRONT	Y	192.168.100.34	234.1.0.34

PT-JOY-G2	BROADCAST AREA		192.168.100.35	N/A
TRICASTER TC1	BROADCAST AREA	N/A	192.168.100.113	N/A
PT12X-SDI-WH-G2	CHURCH SIDE	Y	192.168.100.41	234.1.0.41
PT20X-SDI-WH-G2	CHURCH SIDE	Y	192.168.100.42	234.1.0.42
MAC MINI	FRONT STAGE	N/A	192.168.100.43	N/A
INTEL NUC	LOBBY	N/A	192.168.100.44	N/A
IP Joystick	2nd Floor		192.168.100.51	N/A

In the diagram above, we can see that there are 6 multicasts enabled PTZOptics cameras. Because these cameras are enabled for multicast, the video feeds can be accessed simultaneously by multiple computers on your network. Therefore, we can do things like setting up a second computer dedicated to a production made for a Spanish audience. Perhaps, we have a translator providing Spanish translated audio available to our 2nd live streaming computer. We can also simultaneously have a camera operator pulling in the video feeds along with an overflow display in another room.

The IP address table above also includes information about the device's multicast addresses. Multicast addresses can range from 224.0.0.0 to 239.255.255.255. If you want to leverage the power of multicast video, you must remember to select networking equipment that can support multicast network traffic. Also, remember that each video device that you plan to use will require its own multicast address. Notice that each camera has a unique IP address and a unique multicast address.

Finally, when you are selecting a network switch to be used for the NewTek NDI, we highly suggest considering a switch that meets all of the following requirements. You may want to set up a dedicated network just for your IP video sources especially if this is the first IP based video production system you have setup ever.

- Gigabit Ethernet * Required*
- Full Throughput Switch Backplane *Required*
- DHCP Recommended
- For Devices That Optionally Support PoE
    o PTZOptics NDI | HX Cams require PoE (15.4w)
    o NewTek Connect Spark requires PoE (15w)
    o Note* PoE+ supports PoE, but PoE doesn't support PoE+
    o Make a note of the power needed for devices/switch

IF YOU ARE USING A MANAGED SWITCH

Managed switches are great, but the settings need to be tweaked to accommodate low latency IP based video for production. You can use almost any Gigabit managed switch that meets the requirements above, but you will also have to disable a few settings and enable Flow Control as Asymmetrical.

- Disable Quality of Service
- Disable Jumbo Frames
- Enable Flow Control as Asymmetrical of Simply as On
- Enable IGMP Snooping if Using Multicast (mDNS)
- Configure IGMP Querier and Query Interval Per Switch in Multi-Switch Networks (While Using Multicast)

DEALING WITH FIREWALLS

- mDNS must be accessible
- Manual discover requires access to port 5960 for messaging and all coming after 5961 for streams
- Check the port range from Microsoft PC's using Cmd: **ntsh**

NETWORK ADAPTERS

- Use DHCP to assign IP addresses or assign static manually
- Use manual configuration in NDI Access Manager to cross subnets
- Designate network location on all NICs as Work (private)
- Connect and available Gigabit + network interfaces

A little bit on latency

- Full circle latency must be <14ms
- NDI v3.5 supports UDP with Forward Error Correction for unicast (prior versions use TCP)

If this all looks like another language, please don't worry. I have an entire course on church video production, and the NewTek NDI linked below. If you already have an IT person that you work with, these are important requirements you may want them to consider. It's likely that you already have a networking system in place. If you want to leverage that system as a video distribution network, you may need to configure some of the network settings.

Free Course on the NewTek NDI - https://www.udemy.com/newtek-ndi/

14 WHAT YOU SHOULD KNOW ABOUT POWER OVER ETHERNET

Guest Chapter by Tyler Andrews CEO of PoE Texas

I'll start by saying that I love Power Over Ethernet (PoE). Yeah, yeah, it's what I do for a living, but, really, how cool is it that you can take the ethernet cable you have in your wall and get it to power up cameras, iPads, or even TV's? I see PoE as Potential (#volts - okay, yeah, I couldn't resist the nerd joke, and be forewarned they keep coming).

In all seriousness, though, Power Over Ethernet can save you 30% on any given project where you would otherwise have to call a licensed electrician out to pull a permit just to put an outlet somewhere so that you can hang a camera. Even better, because PoE runs on low voltage power (think closer to the battery for your kids' toys), you can safely do the work yourself, or at least get your techie nephew to do it. If it's so cool, why doesn't everyone do this all the time? Frankly, I'm stumped. However, I blame it on it sounding too technical because it has to do with computers talking to each other.

That ends today. I help a lot of people find the right PoE solution and believe me when I say you can understand PoE. Once you have a few basic terms and principles, you'll blow minds! To make that magic happen for you, I will simplify Power Over Ethernet (PoE) in an easy to understand way even if you've never worked on a network before.

Let's start with a pronunciation guide. This is worth your time.

PoE – pronounced *PEE – OH – EEE*. Not like Edgar Allan "Poe."

IEEE 802.3af – pronounced *EYE TRIPLE EEEE EIGHT OH TWO DOT THREE AYE EF.*

Okay, so say it with me now . . . EYE TRIPLE EEEE EIGHT OH TWO DOT THREE AYE EF.

Great work!!

So, what does that all mean? Working from the ground up, PoE means putting electricity onto an ethernet cable along with a data signal. You can use that electricity to power all kinds of things: cameras, lights, wifi access points, iPads, phones, TV's, computers, media players, Raspberry Pis and much more. Warning: once you get into what you can power with PoE, it goes deep, like X-Files deep.

Oh, about the IEEE thing (yeah, you heard how cool you sound saying it). Simply put, you have a very smart guy like Paul making cameras, and you have another smart guy like me – *ahem, why thank you* – making devices that can power those devices over a network cable. To make sure we all work together without having to fight over things constantly, we called our friends at the Institute of Electrical and Electronics Engineers (IEEE – "EYE TRIPLE EEE") and asked them to help us create a standard way of doing things. They agreed and added us to the 802nd section part three subsection "af" of their standard. You don't need to read it, but if you do – SPOILER ALERT – data and power get together by the end. That standard is how Paul and I agree on how the PoE will work, so we both make devices that talk the same PoE.

As time passed, we kept coming up with better and better ideas, like MORE POWER! So now we have a few more standards. Here's a table of the PoE standards as they stand today (don't worry,

I will explain it all so bask in the glory of it): *Passive PoE can operate anywhere from 12 volts up to 58 volts. You'll want to check your specifications carefully to make sure they match your device.*

The real

Camera & Lens			Rear Board	
Video Sensor	1/2.7" CMOS, 2.12 Mega Pixels		Video Output	HDMI, 3G-SDI, IP Streaming, CVBS
Frame Rates	1080p/60, 50, 30 & 25, 1080/60 & 50, 720p/60, 50, 30 & 25		Network Interface	RJ45
			Audio Interface	Line In, 3.5mm (HDMI & IP Stream Only)
Frame Rates (CVBS)	576i/30, 480i/30		Communication	RS-232, RS-485, PELCO-D/P,
Focal Length	12x, F3.5mm-42.3mm, F1.8-F2.8		Baud Rate	2400/4800/9600 bits
Lens Zoom	12x		Power Supply	JEITA type Power Adapter (DC IN 12V)
Field of View	72.5°		SDI Interface	BNC – 75 Ohm, Female
Min Lux	0.5 Lux at F1.8, AGC ON		0 Interface	Future Use
Shutter Speed	1/30s - 1/10000s		**Electrical Index**	
SNR	>55dB		Power Supply	12W (Max)
Vertical Flip & Mirror	Supported		Input Voltage	12V DC (10.8 - 13.0V DC) or PoE 802.3af
Horizontal Angle of View	6.9° (tele) to 72.5° (wide)			
Vertical Angle of View	3.9° (tele) to 44.8°(wide)		**Physical**	
Working Environment	Indoor		Dimension (in.)	5.6W x 6.5H x 6.7D (7.88H max w/ Tilt)
			Dimensions (mm)	142W x 164H x 169D (189H max w/ Tilt)
Pan & Tilt Movement			Box Dimensions	9"x9"x10"	229mmx254mmx229mm
Pan Movement	±170°		Camera Weight	3.05 lbs. (1.38 kg)
Tilt Rotation	Up: 90°, Down: 30°		Boxed Weight	5.4 lbs. (2.45 kg)
Presets	10 via IR (255 via Serial or IP)			

difference between the types of PoE is how much power your devices need in Watts. What you need to know is that the watts are how much power a device consumes to do its job. The last column shows you the kind of devices each power level can support.

And that, my friends, is all you need to know. Seriously. When it's all said and done, you just need to make sure you pick a Powered Device (PD) like a camera or media controller that matches the standard of the Power Sourcing Equipment (PSE). You like how I snuck . . . sneaked . . . er . . . Snooked some more vocabulary in there?

"But how do I do that?" you ask. I'll break it down bullet point style. Let's say you're looking to add a new camera or any device to your network.

➤ First, go find the datasheet. Don't Panic. Every engineer makes a datasheet because it's their way of bragging. It's like they are street racers with their tricked-out muscle cars, they

want you to know what they've got under the hood.
Typically, you can find PoE in the Electrical section. You'll
find something like "POE" or "IEEE 802.3 af". That tells
you what kind of PoE your new toy has.

➤ Second, select a type of Power Sourcing Equipment (PoE),
that's your PoE switch or midspan (injector). What's a switch
and what's a midspan you ask? They look a lot alike but
don't be fooled. They're different animals with different
purposes like a king snake and a coral snake (Krykie, she's a
beauty! I'm going to pick her up!).

➤ A PoE Switch adds power and routes data between devices.
One data connection in, multiple ports of power and data
out.

➤ A Midspan is an additional PoE source that can be used in
combination with an existing PoE or non-PoE network
switch.

 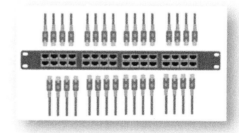

Why use a Midspan when I can just buy a switch?

There are two situations where a midspan injector makes more sense:

1) Let's say you have your network all set up, and it's working great. All the ports are forwarding, Quality of Service (QoS) is great, and everything has been working for a while. If you're like me, the guy who set up the network has gone all Jason Bourne on me which means I'll never find him again. Then you need to add PoE to it, or you need to add PoE+ to your PoE switch because you need that little extra power. Do I want to try to pull out that switch that I paid a lot of money and headache to get configured to add a few PoE+ devices? At this point, it's not about the money; it's about the headache of nothing working for a month while we get it all sorted out again. Or do I add a midspan in a few minutes and forget about it.

2) You don't want to have to buy a switch that doesn't have the features you want just because it can do the PoE you want. We see this more often than you'd think. For example, you have an NDI switch that doesn't have PoE or doesn't do PoE+. You need that PoE power for your streaming camera. Do you buy an NDI switch that may be way more than you need with PoE+ or use a midspan to add it to the switch you know and love?

➤ Finally, once you know your switch or midspan is compatible, then make sure you have enough ports and power budget for all your PoE devices on your PSE. Most switches and some midspans don't have enough total power budget to give you full PoE power on all ports at the same time. Why?! you may ask. It comes down to cost and how much you'll use each port. Your Toyota Corolla technically *can* go to 120 mph, but you use it to get to work and back. If you wanted to go 120 mph, you upgrade a Porsche or Corvette or something truly awesome.

There's a catch . . . This part takes . . . *Gasp*. . . Math. I know you swore you would never touch a calculator again when you got out of school. Believe me. It's not that bad.

Simple Method:

Add up all the rated power consumption of all the devices and compare it to the rated power of your PSE. For example:

2 x PTZ Optics cameras at 12 watts each = 24 watts

2 x Polycom Phones at 6 watts each = 12 watts

Nerdy Method
I couldn't leave you with it that simple. If you'd really like to get details, you can use our PoE Calculator to estimate how much you can expect in cable loss as well!

1 x High-End Wifi Access Point (WAP) = 23 watts

All together: 24 + 12 + 23 = 59 watts

> ➤ You need at least 5 ports and a total of 60 watts. Oh, and by the way, you need PoE+ for that high-end WAP.

If you find yourself saying, I'm not going to remember all that! Don't. Just remember to come back to your book here to find a link to a handy tool to walk you through your PSE selection process. You can find it in our PoE PM Work Book – 101_(Included as a resource inside the Church Streaming Udemy Course).

E voila! That covered what you need to know. You now know more than 90% of people in the world do about Power Over Ethernet. With this simple set of tools, you'll shock yourself (please only figuratively) with what you can accomplish and how easily it will happen. Put that 30% you saved on an electrician into a new rocking set of drums or your kid's college fund, whatever you think is most important. Whether you decide to tackle a project yourself or hire someone else, you now have the core knowledge you need to handle a Power Over Ethernet projects.

I will close with the immortal words of Stan Lee, "With great power comes great responsibility." Pro Tip: whatever you do, do not put on a blonde mullet wig, don a furry pair of briefs, and hold up a sword shouting, "I have the POWER!". It never turns out the way you think it will. Best of luck with your Live Streaming!

15 WHY YOUR CHURCH SHOULD START A PODCAST

Podcasts are an incredibly popular way of listening to audio content. In this chapter, we will talk about why so many churches are starting podcasts. One of the best things about starting a podcast is that it's incredibly affordable to get started. Most churches already have high-quality audio systems in place to amplify the voices of their speakers inside the church. The churches audio system can easily be used to record services and upload them as a podcast.

For members and nonmembers of the church alike, listening to a podcast is convenient. Many people subscribe to a podcast they are interested in on their smartphones. In this way, they can easily listen in their car, on a jog, or while they're shopping in the grocery store. Podcasting is a form of internet radio that benefits from having a host and a moderator. Popular religious podcasts that I listen to regularly include World Religion News and Christianity Today. These podcasts talk about important issues happening outside the church. They keep listeners informed on issues in the world at large through the lens of

Christianity. Churches can use podcasting to reach new members in a variety of ways. The easiest way for a church to get started is to record their Sunday services with an audio program such as Audacity. Audacity is a free audio recording software available on both Mac and PCs. All you need to do is plug your digital audio mixer into your audio recording computer with a USB cable to

CHURCH
Pro Video Tip

Podcasts are a great way to reach out to millenials. Consider subscribing to a local church's podcast. I highly recommend the Dare to Imagine church podcast along with Christianity Today.

record the audio. If your digital audio mixer does not include a USB output, you can purchase an inexpensive USB audio interface that costs only $35 from Behringer. This equipment can be used to record the entire sermon but also the intro and outro segments for a higher quality production podcast. You can use your USB audio interface to capture audio from your larger audio mixer but also to bring in an XLR microphone into your computer for podcasting. You can start and end your podcasts with custom segments and paste in various parts of the recorded service's audio in post-production.

For example, someone from your church in the media team may want to include an introduction to each podcast to explain some of the important information and context for the church service that has been recorded. Perhaps the podcast moderator will include the podcast title, the episode number, and some brief information on how podcast listeners can get in contact with the church. The amazing thing about church media and outreach programs is that the church is a real place. People can reach out to you whenever they feel compelled to do so. Reaching new members and people who need the message of God with live streaming and podcasting can be the simple push people need to bring their lives closer to God.

Once your church has recorded a podcast, it's time to post your podcast to the world using a podcast hosting service. There are free podcast hosting services available such a SoundCloud, and there are premium podcast hosting services such as Podbean. Here at StreamGeeks, we use Podbean because it also includes the ability to host video podcasts. Once your podcast is available via a hosting service, it is automatically shared with the world's largest podcast delivery networks such as iTunes, Spotify, Stitcher Radio and more. This is a powerful way to connect your churches podcast to the world in a very simple, easy to manage workflow. Each week when your podcast is ready, you can upload it to your hosting service, and within minutes your podcast will be available to all your listeners.

Here at The StreamGeeks, we are always interested to know who our podcast listeners are and if our content is important to them. We regularly remind podcast listeners to reach out and let us know what they find most interesting. You would be surprised how effective simply asking podcast listeners to follow you on social media is. Consider asking your listeners to reach out to you with a phone call. Here are a couple of tips you can use to increase the effectiveness of your church's podcast.

First, always make a brief introduction to the subject matter of your podcast. As you introduce your podcast content, this is a great chance to thank those who donate to your church and potential sponsors. If your church has a program that you think podcast listeners may be interested in, this is a great time to review your seasonal offerings with listeners. Depending on how much production your podcast requires, you may want to consider using sound effects and breaking up the service into **specific bite-size chunks**. Maybe your **podcast moderators like to reflect on certain portions of the church service** throughout the podcast. This is a great way to provide additional value for listeners and even members who attended the church service, who can benefit from additional reflection. It's always important to **put yourself in the shoes of the listener** and imagine where the podcast listener might be. Many podcast listeners like to listen to podcasts as they drive to work. Using this perspective can help your podcast moderator prepare content that is more engaging and relevant to listeners. Finally, consider a **call to action at the end of each podcast**. This is your chance to ask your listeners to take action. Perhaps you'd like to suggest listeners donate to your church. Whatever your church's goals are, a podcast is a great outlet for delivering value and promotion activities.

In conclusion, podcasting is an easy way for your church to deliver your sermons online. Every year there are more and more podcast listeners, looking for local, personalized audio content that can help them feel part of their community. The great thing about podcasting for houses of worship is the fact that **most churches already have all the audio equipment they need** to produce a high-quality experience for listeners. **Podcasting is a great segue into live streaming** and podcasting can be available via video as well. Adding video to your Podcasts can create a visual bridge into your church and help people connect with the people in your church who are delivering your message. Whether you choose to add a visual component to your podcast or not this is a great opportunity to **provide additional reflection and context for your service**. You may find dedicated church members can get even more each week out of your services, and potential members can better understand their open invitation to your church. Podcasting is a great way to connect with your community and build your online presence in a convenient modern way. Podcasting is a fun and creative way to share your church's latest programs and offerings with the world. Finally, with a little thought, your church can craft a podcast that furthers your core mission and increases donations.

Why your church should start a podcast

1.   It is an easy way to deliver your sermons to members who couldn't make it or potential members online

2.   You already have the equipment you need

3.   Podcasting is an easy way to provide additional reflection and context for your sermon

4.   Great way to connect with your community and build your online presence

Want to learn more?

Use Coupon Code "StreamGeek" to take my complete course on setting up a podcast at your church. Course link is available here: https://www.udemy.com/live-streaming-a-podcast

16 WHAT'S NEXT?

When I first started writing this book, I was compelled to help connect my wife with her hometown church. I wanted to create a book for Pastor Golden that could guide him through the opportunities he would unlock with his new live streaming system. I understood that online media would be foreign territory for most ministry leaders. I set out to create something that would update church leaders on all things live streaming. I also created an online training course to accompany this book, for the volunteers and church media leaders alike. As time went on, I began to further my understanding of how live church services are touching the lives of people around the world. I love to hear from people like Tori Parker who watched the Olivet United Methodist Church's candlelight service on her couch as she healed from surgery this Christmas season. It warms my heart to hear from people like Mrs. Agnes Miner who thanks God for the chance to watch a church service from her hometown that she has moved away from more than 40 years ago.

As our culture's communication trends continue to shift, live streaming will become an increasingly powerful tool for the church. I'm honored to be part of a movement that brings people together to worship both online and in person. I believe churches will see the importance of online communications grow with each coming year.

If you have any questions about a topic covered in this book, please feel free to email me at paul.richards@streamgeeks.us. The best way to get advice on a technology related question is to create a post in our "Churches That Live Stream" Facebook Group. It's here where you can find hundreds of other ministry leaders talking about how they are leveraging the power of live streaming for the ultimate commission.

I hope that this book has prepared you with the knowledge you need to get started using live streaming to spread the message of God. The best tip inside this book is encouraging your team to ask for advice from local worship leaders. I highly suggest seeking out other churches in your area. Make a phone call and see if you can join them for a Sunday service.

Again, please feel free to reach out to our community Facebook User Group found at https://facebook.com/groups/church-streamers.

If you are ready to continue your learning you can register for our online training course here: https://www.udemy.com/church-streaming/.

God Bless,

Paul Richards
Chief Streaming Officer
StreamGeeks
Email: paul.richards@streamgeeks.us

GLOSSARY OF TERMS

3.5mm Audio Cable - Male to male stereo cable, common in standard audio uses.

4K - A high definition resolution option (3840 x 2160 pixels or 4096 x 2160 pixels)

16:9 [16x9] - Aspect ratio of 9 units of height and 16 units of width. Used to describe standard HDTV, Full HD, non-HD digital television and analog widescreen television.

API [Application Program Interface]- A streaming API is a set of data a social media network uses to transmit on the web in real time. Going live directly from YouTube or Facebook uses their API.

Bandwidth - Bandwidth is measured in bits and the word "bandwidth" is used to describe the maximum data transfer rate.

Bitrate – Bitrates are used to select the data transfer size of your live stream. This is the number of bits per second that can be transmitted along a digital network.

Broadcasting - The distribution of audio or video content to a dispersed audience via any electronic mass communications medium.

Broadcast Frame Rates - Used to describe how many frames per second are captured in broadcasting. Common frame rates in broadcast include **29.97fps and 59.97 fps**.

Capture Card - A device with inputs and outputs that allow a camera to connect to a computer.

Chroma Key - A video effect that allows you to layer images and manipulate color hues [i.e. green screen] to make a subject transparent.

Cloud Based-Streaming - Streaming and video production interaction that occurs within the cloud, therefore accessible beyond a single user's computer device.

Color Matching - The process of managing color and lighting settings on multiple cameras to match their appearance.

Community Strategy - The strategy of building one's brand and product recognition by building meaningful relationships with an audience, partner, and clientele base.

Content Delivery Network [CDN] - A network of servers that deliver web-based content to an end user.

CPU [Central Processing Unit] – This is the main processor inside of your computer, and it is used to run the operating system and your live streaming software.

DAW - Digital Audio Workstation software is used to produce music. It can also be used to interface with multiple devices and other software using MIDI.

DB9 Cable - A common cable connection for camera joystick serial control.

DHCP [Dynamic Host Configuration Protocol] Router - A router with a network management protocol that dynamically sets IP addresses, so the server can communicate with its sources.

Encoder - A device or software that converts your video sources into an RTMP stream. The RTMP stream can be delivered to CDNs such as Facebook or YouTube.

FOH – Front of House is the part of your church that is open to the public. There is generally a FOH audio mix made to fill this space with the appropriate audio.

GPU – Graphics Processing Unit. This is your graphics card which is used for handling video inside your computer.

H.264 & H.265 - Common formats of video recording, compression, and delivery.

HDMI [High Definition Multimedia Interface] - A cable commonly used for transmitting audio/video.

HEVC [High Efficiency Video Coding] - H.265, is an advanced version of h.264 which promises higher efficiency but lacks the general support of h.264 among most software and hardware solutions available today.

IP [Internet Protocol] Camera/Video - A camera or video source that can send and receive information via a network & internet.

IP Control - The ability to control/connect a camera or device via a network or internet.

ISP – Internet Service Provider. This is the company that you pay monthly for your internet service. They will provide you with your internet connection and router.

Latency - The time it takes between sending a signal and the recipient receiving it.

Live Streaming - The process of sending and receiving audio and or video over the internet.

LAN [Local Area Network] - A network of computers linked together in one location.

MIDI [Musical Instrument Digital Interface] - A way to connect a sound or action to a device. (i.e. a keyboard or controller to trigger an action or sound on a stream

Multicast - Multicast is a method of sending data to multiple computers on your LAN without incurring additional bandwidth for each receiver. Multicast is very different from Unicast which is a data transport method that opens a unique stream of data between each sender and receiver. Multicast allows you to broadcast video from a single camera or live streaming computer to multiple destinations inside your church without adding the bandwidth burden on your network.

Multicorder – Also known as an "IsoCorder" is a feature of streaming software that allows the user to record raw footage from camera feed directly to your hard drive. This feature allows you to record multiple video sources at the same time.

NDI® [Network Device Interface] - Software standard developed by NewTek to enable video-compatible products to communicate, deliver, and receive broadcast quality video in high quality, low latency manner that is frame-accurate and suitable for switching in a live production environment.

NDI® Camera - A camera that allows you to send and receive video over your LAN using NDI technology.

NDI® | HX - NDI High Efficiency, optimizes NDI for limited bandwidth environments.

Network - A digital telecommunications network which allows nodes to share resources. In computer networks, computing devices exchange data with each other using connections between nodes.

Network Switch – A network switch is a networking device that connects multiple devices on a computer network using packet switching to receive, process and forward data to the destination device.

NTSC - Video standard used in North America.

OBS – Open Broadcaster Software is one of the industries most popular live streaming software solutions because it is completely free. OBS is available for Mac, PC, and Linux computers.

PAL - Analog video format commonly used outside of North America.

PCIe- Allows for high bandwidth communication between a device and the computer's motherboard. A PCIe card can installed inside a custom-built computer to provide multiple video inputs (such as HDMI or SDI).

PoE - Power over Ethernet.

PTZ - Pan, tilt, zoom.

RS-232 - Serial camera control transmission.

Router – Your internet router is generally provided to you by your internet service provider. This device may include a firewall, WiFi and/or network switch functionality. This device connects your network to the internet.

RTMP [Real Time Messaging Protocol] – Used for live streaming your video over the public internet.

RTSP [Real Time Streaming Protocol] - Network control protocol for streaming from one point to point. Generally, used for transporting video inside your local area network.

vMix® – vMix is a live streaming software built for Windows computers. It is a professional favorite with high-end features such as low latency capture, NDI support, instant replay, multi-view and much more.

Wirecast® – Wirecast is a live streaming software available for both Mac and PCs with advanced features such as five layers of overlays, lower thirds, virtual sets and much more.

xSplit® – xSplit is a live streaming software with a free and/or low monthly fee paid option. This is a great software available on for Windows computers that combines advanced features and simple to use interface.

About the Author

Paul is the Chief Streaming Officer for StreamGeeks. StreamGeeks is a group of video production experts dedicated to helping organizations discover the power of live streaming.

Every Monday, Paul and his team produce a live show in their downtown West Chester, Pennsylvania studio location. Having produced live shows as amateurs themselves, the StreamGeeks steadily worked their way to a professional level by learning from experience as they went.

Today, they have an impressive following and a tight-knit online community which they serve through consultations and live shows that continue to inspire, motivate, and inform organizations who refuse to settle for mediocrity. The show explores the ever-evolving broadcast and live streaming market while engaging a dedicated live audience.

As a husband and father raising his children in the Lutheran faith, Richards knows a thing or two about the technology inside the church. Richards now specializes in the live streaming media industry leveraging the technology for lead generation. In his book, "Live Streaming is Smart Marketing", Richards reveals his view on lead generation and social media.

Additional Online Courses:

Join over 20,000 other students learning how to leverage the power of live streaming! Take the following courses taught by Paul Richards for free by downloading the course coupon codes available at streamgeeks.us/start.

- **Facebook Live Streaming** - *Beginner*

This course will take your through the Facebook Live basics. It has already been updated twice! This also includes using Facebook Live Reactions!

- **YouTube Live Streaming** - *Beginner*

This course will take you through the YouTube Live basics. It also includes essential branding and tips for marketing.

- **Introduction to OBS (Open Broadcaster Software)**

This course will take your through one of the world's most popular FREE live streaming software solutions. OBS is a great place to start live streaming for free!

- **Introduction to xSplit Software** - *Beginner*

This course takes you through xSplit which has more features that OBS but costs roughly $5/month. Learn how to create amazing live productions and make videos much faster with xSplit!

- **Introduction to vMix** - *Intermediate*

vMix will have you live streaming like the Pros in no time. This Windows based software will amaze even the most advanced video producers!

- **Introduction to Wirecast** - *Intermediate*

Wirecast is the preferred software for so many professional live streamers. Available for Mac or PC this is the ideal software for anyone looking for professional streaming.

- **Introduction to NewTek NDI** - *Intermediate*

NewTek's innovative IP video standard NDI (Network Device Interface) will change the way you think about live video production. Learn how to use this innovative new technology for live streaming and video production system design.

- **Introduction to live streaming course** - *Beginner*

This course includes everything you need to get started designing your show. This course includes a starter pack of course files including: Photoshop, After Effects and free Virtual Sets.

- **Introduction to live streaming** - *Intermediate*

This course focuses on more advanced techniques for optimizing your production workflow and using compression to get the most out of your processor. This course includes files for: Photoshop, After Effects and free Virtual Sets.

- **Live Streaming for Good - Church Streaming Course** - *Intermediate*

This course focuses on live streaming for churches and houses of worship. We tackle some of the big questions about live streaming in a house of worship and dive into the specific challenges of this space.

- **How to Live Streaming A Wedding** - *Beginner*

This is a great course for anyone looking to start live streaming weddings. Originally designed for Wedding Photographers to add a live streaming service to their existing portfolio of offerings. This course is great for beginners